A Blackman's Connection to God through the Blackwoman

A Blackman's Connection to God through the Blackman
& the Implications of Divine Spiritual Principles
Urban Cries
Volume 2

First published in 2008 by TamaRe House Publishers Ltd, UK
www.tamarehouse.com
info@tamarehouse.com
+44 207 9788321

Printed and Bound by Lightning Source, UK

Authored by Paul Simons aka Nebu Ka Ma'at

Copyright © 2007 Paul Simons

All rights are reserved. No part of this book are to be reprinted, copied or stored in retrieval systems of any type, except by written permission from the Author. Parts of this book may however be used only in reference to support related documents or subjects.

ISBN: 978-1-906169-07-7

Contents

Dedications and Acknowledgements   3
Preface and Introduction   5

Part_1

A Man's Connection to God through his Woman

1- Urban Cries – *What do we want?*   15
    ; Un-break my heart   17
    ; Connecting with God   25
2- The Hip-Hop & RnB Culture – *Show and tell!*   29
    ; The Aesthetics of Hip-Hop   33
    ; The deepest part of being Human   38

Part_2

The Science of Love in the Making
– *Revised* –

3- Impulsive behaviour…   45
    ; Sexual Energy   46
    ; Sexual Mantras   48
4- Love in Creational myths   52
    ; Yin and Yang   53
    ; Aphrodite and Venus   55
    ; Love and Sex in the Sumerian epics   57
    ; Egiptian Viagra   59
5- Compatibility and Relationships   61
    ; The feeling of Love   63
    ; Choosing a mate or partner   66
    ; Communication with Love   71
    ; Sex Magic   74
6- Love and Relationship Archetypes   79
    ; Daddy's girl and Mummy's boy   80
    ; The Shadow and Persona   81

7-	Love in Afrokhan Culture	84
	; The Philosophy of Love	84

Part_3

144,000 Souls of Spiritual Nostalgia

8-	In Conclusion	89
	; The Science of E-Motion	89
	; The Ultimate Observer	95
	; Final Acknowledgements	99
	; A New Beginning	102
9-	Keeping the Passion Alive	105

Appendix

A – The Law of One, & Interconnectedness	115
B – The Law of Intention, & Karma	116
C – The Law of Projection, & Attraction	117
D – The Law of Grace, & Mercy	118
E – The Law of Responsibility, & Godliness	119
F – The Law of Integrity, & Manifestation	120
G – The Law of Unconditional Love	121
H – Afrokhan	122
I – AfroCentricity	123
J – The Chakras	124

Index   128

Dedications and Acknowledgements

This work is a dedication to, and is an acknowledgement of, the women of my life who have established a particular significance. It is my admission, therefore, that it is the women of my life that have given me the greatest lessons in life and living. Through the Blackwoman, in particular, I have learnt not just how to be a man, but what it means to be a Blackman and what my obligations thereof are within the modern world. Indeed, I have learned how to connect to the Creator using the Power and magic of Love.

So, thanks to the following women for giving me their time and energy. Without all of you I would not be the man that I am today and am still becoming.

Hidiatu
Desiree
Nadia
Louise
Marian
Gill
Angie
Hazel
Millie
Patricia

Preface and Introduction

It was just before sunrise when I was suddenly awoken by the yelling. I remember because I usually awake from my sleep to a bright and fully present morning. I also recall not hearing the beautiful singing of the early morning birds, as they were the day before, and the days before that. So, this morning was very different in a number of ways; different enough to make me think for a second that maybe this is all just a dream.

The voices rose higher and higher in volume, and in such a way that scared me to trembles and sweats. Unable to actually understand or make sense of what the fuss was about, my feelings told me it definitely wasn't good. Sure I had heard yelling and shouting coming from these same two persons before, but this was different, significantly. But what was I to do? What was to be done or said that would stop this painfully uncomfortable situation, of which I was helpless? My fear had graduated from myself to a fear for the woman, whose voice was all too familiar. I became afraid for her.

She was screaming; she was upset; she was crying and her tone of voice was of one which was begging to be free of this torture. The tone of voice was by far different from anything I had ever heard coming from the woman. It did not compare to the way she was the previous evening, as she was laying the table for dinner. Her angry voice did not match the smile I was remembering of her from the night before. What had happened?

I was limited in view to what was going on. There was something blocking my view, a huge bedspread I think, or something of equal size. This was very unusual. I was used to waking up with complete view of the room. I would grab onto the railings of my crib as I pulled myself up to stand, and to look over into the vastness of the outer space. But this time I was bothered with what I might see if I stood up. I was worried that the man with the deep voice would turn and start yelling at me for waking too early. So, I lay still and waited.

Then before I knew it, all attention was on me. The woman's voice had changed from *fear* to *love* as she leaned over my crib to adjust my coverings. At my age at the time, the situation was nothing but confusion. How was she able to switch moods, in such a flash? Where did the man disappear and go?

In my later years, actually, just last year (2006), I learned of a chemical hormone present within the brain. It is the hormone Oxytocin. This chemical is one that creates affinity between two individuals; in this case we speak of that between mother and foetus. From as early as weeks into the pregnancy, providing the mother is actually aware of the pregnancy; the pituitary gland releases this hormone into the bloodstream. It creates specific nervous responses within the body, which throws the woman into love and devotion of the unborn child. Like an addiction. But also like a protective mechanism that is vital, and in order for the growth and development of the foetus to be nurtured appropriately.

This creates a cohesive mother—child or child—mother corporeal attachment, before birth, which, for the child is actually its first significant relationship.

But where does the affinity of men (fathers) fit into this equation?

Preface and Introduction

The short, eventful story above provides insight to a few basic spiritual laws and principles: firstly, the 'Law of Unconditional Love,' and secondly, the psychological principles of affinity. It demonstrates how one can transform their own state of mind in an instant, by way of emotional and biological association, with persons, places, things or circumstances and so on. This book therefore, is intended to establish seven of such laws, and to place them within specific contexts with which the reader may be able to relate, either through their own experiences or from the experiences of others.

On the subject of love and relationships, there seems to be a negative stigma concerning men, Black men in particular. Let's think about this for a moment.

We often hear the cliché that: "men cannot be trusted;" or, "they only think about one thing;" or, that "all men are dogs." Some would even go as far as saying: "there can never be any such thing as a loyal man." If there were to be broadly accepted scenarios such as these, the possibility of beautiful relationships will become non-existent. Meaning, if we mentally accept these statements as truths, we will inevitably create and experience exactly that. Not to say that some women do not actually experience these emotionally draining circumstances, but to say that all men cannot be trusted is just as ridiculing as saying all women are loyal. To say that all men only think about what they can get from a woman, whether it is sex, money, or someone to replace mum, is as far from reality as saying women do not want anything from a man, except for him to be loving and loyal. No need to further mention the 'dog' scenario here – your imagination is broad enough to see the reciprocal.

"What do we actually want?" is the question here. It is my belief that everyone deserves the best of what they strive for. I mean, it is very easy for one to say: "I want to find the perfect partner," but are we looking at our own selves in terms of becoming the perfect partner? The majority of us aren't.

The type of person we end up with in our relationships is usually directly proportional to the type of person we actually are. I found this to be true in my own experiences. 'Like-minds attract' they say. The 'Law of Projection and Attraction' provides insight to this, and proves to be true regardless of the kind of relationship; whether it is a love relationship, a business relationship, or, simply our friendships.

If I were to put myself into the spotlight and ask myself the question of "what do I want?" The answer would be different on several levels. For instance, my ideas of the perfect relationship when I was a child were based on what I saw on television; the impositions of soap operas, as well as many-a black-and-white film. As a child, back in Jamaica where I was born, I remember watching the old black-and-white movies of the fifties and sixties. I used to take-on the contents of these televised love relationships; I would place them within my own context, and visually project them to a future *me* of much later years. I would literally visualise myself as experiencing these exact stories as a grown up, in my own future. As I grew older though – and after witnessing the split-up of my parents – my ideals changed. Marriage was to be looked at as a possibility to be considered extremely carefully before doing. I became aware that marriage is not always as idealistic as the movies would portray.

Preface and Introduction

Through the cultures of Hip-Hop and R&B, (through what is presented in 'Urban Cries volume 1') I began to get a glimpse of a different reality. I found out through the many genres of Black music that there is a different set of realities that are more real; and that the impositions of televised ideals are almost completely unrealistic and are therefore false impressions.

Prior to becoming aware of the Hip-Hop culture, its messages and musical influences, what I had earlier witnessed of my own mother and father was unfortunately far from ideal also. My father was evidently very abusive to my mother. I hated that, hated him; Errol. I always said to myself that I would never treat women that way. Well, life has since presented me with pressing opportunities to exercise control of my anger and emotions. On a few occasions, I had lost it.

Was this a genetic trait inherited from my father, or was I fully responsible for those actions? Did I create the circumstances that led up to my lashing out, or was it someone else's cause? Why wasn't my first, second or third relationship perfect, since I had already envisioned what it would look like from an early age?

These are some of the questions this small book will answer; through the examples of my own experiences and from learning of the experiences of others. I should point out that I have never been anywhere as outlandish as with my father's treatment of my mother but to say that I have grown to become a very caring and loving person, generally speaking. I have re-established the possibility of settling down and getting married, which I at least attempted. So now, here's the funny thing, It must have been the shortest marriage in history. The rapid breakdown of my marriage threw me into a place of: 'keeping myself protected from falling in love and 'finding it difficult to open up to prospective partners and to let love in;' and I would try to align myself with impossible relationships.

My lifetime experience of love and relationships has been an adventurous *meantime* education, in terms of using myself as an example in order to inspire others. Not to say that it was perfect, but to say it involved a bit of every kind of emotion. Through trial and error, so to say, I would quickly learn what works versus what doesn't work. Moreover, I am a firm believer in learning from my mistakes. I believe that there is no such thing as a bad experience, and as long as we learn from the events of our lives, we can consider them as learning stages of life.

This book is written in an attempt to reach and inspire the young people of the UK (United Kingdom – England), into feeling the possibility of creating and having very powerful love relationships. The 'Urban Cries' series of books is designed to present simple but powerful 'Mental-Technology' tools, in which young people of the Reggae, Hip-Hop and R&B cultures can consciously utilise to achieve a spiritually richer, fuller and more productive life. This volume of 'Urban Cries,' is based around the subject of Love and relationships; with insights to 'A Blackman's Connection to God through the Blackwoman within the Music culture.' The first two chapters (Part_1) provide an insight into the generalised expectations of what love and relationships are about, from the perspectives of the Hip-Hop & RnB cultures. There we will also look at the 'Seven Laws of Human Inter-relationships,' and emphasise ways that they can be utilised to catapult us into creating long lasting loving relationships. The laws are:

Preface and Introduction

1. The Law of One and Interconnectedness
2. The Law of Intention and Karma
3. The Law of Projection and Attraction
4. The Law of Grace and Mercy
5. The Law of Responsibility and Godliness
6. The Law of Integrity and Manifestation
7. The Law of Unconditional Love

The next 5 chapters (Part_2) are actually a revised version of a chapter within my book, *'The Mystical and Magical Paths of Self and not-self,* Vol.2,' adapted to fit the context of the Reggae, Hip-Hop and RnB communities of the Western world. Part_3, the 8th and 9th chapters, attempts to combine the first and second parts in conclusion.

So without further ado, let us get on with it. Chapter 1 begins with a resounding question

A Blackman's Connection to God through the Blackwoman

Part_1

Paul Simons

A Man's Connection to God through his woman

Ch. 1

Urban Cries
What do we want?

My first significant relationship occurred when I was around the age of fourteen. Her name was Patricia. She was a year older than I was, although her mentality was as though she were in her twenties. She was from a family of five children, of which two siblings were either side of her own age. Having an older brother and sister, (with two younger sisters,) she was, through their influence, a lot more mature than I was. I only had one younger sister (Sarah) living with me who was under two years old at the time. Not much for me to go on, outside of close friends at school, etc. My mother remarried after our coming to England and divorcing my father.

Andrew, Patricia's brother, was heavily into reggae music and had his own sound system, which he used to play at local parties every now and then. My personal interest at the time, as was the case with many of my closer friends, was in the Hip-Hop and Soul genres of music. RnB wasn't such a popular term as it is today, the term 'Rhythm and Blues' would somehow better fit the generation of that time.

However, it was within the context of music, and partying that got Patricia and I involved with each other in the first instance. I mean, our relationship was initially based around our love for music and the desire to go out partying whenever we could. Our parents didn't exactly just let us out whenever, as you can appreciate. But for Pat, it was a lot more than just going out and raving. This sista was in Love. I was her first real love. This frightened me at the time because I had never really experienced what it is like for a girl to be in love with me before. But, the real scare was realising that I wasn't actually in love myself – and of how I could communicate this reality to her.

    She was mentally very strong and a powerful young woman. I mean, her level of communication was phenomenal. She had a way of speaking to people that got her whatever she wanted. Maybe her having an older brother, whom many in the local Peckham community feared, due to his outlandish, gangster-type attitude, influenced this. Needless to say, Pat was able to skilfully hold on to me for up to about one year – with the help of the feared, older brother. I can only imagine what she must be like today (one who pays her own bills and kicks down her own doors; and still waits for her *man* to open doors and pick up the dinner bills).

I say this was my first significant relationship because through the experience, I had learnt how it feels to be loved and cared for (by a girlfriend, that is).

> **Express gratitude and appreciation for the love and adoration received from another. The Universe will increase its loving energy to you through that individual and indeed others**

Pat's tenacity toward maintaining the relationship taught me how to value and fight for the things and the people we love and care for. It was from her that I first heard the words "I love you," which was often followed by, "You don't care about me or anyone but yourself." I obviously did not express my gratitude enough. It is interesting however, that whenever someone accuses us of being non-caring or selfish, that we never actually think of ourselves as being that way before. I mean, it usually seems to be un-intended and thus comes to us as a surprise. But… what is it that drives us to behave in the ways that we do? And… what is it that drives others to interpret us in the way that they do?

Un-break my heart
Through my experiences of love and relationships, I've received the best lessons in life I could ever ask for. However, there was always something missing, a sense that something is not quite right. This feeling tends to create resistance to fully giving our selves to Love. Many whom I have spoken to over the years on the subject would agree. Perhaps you also agree?

> You become what you resist.
> Whatever you resist persists in your life and uses up your energy in struggle.
>
> Diana Cooper

As much as we know what the perfect love relationship ought to look like and feel like, many seem to not get it quite right. There is always something missing. Many of our more serious relationships seem to end with at least one partner having a 'broken-heart'.

I was resisting the love of Patricia, and thus became somewhat un-loving, toward her.

It is natural that as humans, from our youth dream of the perfect relationship – a perfect, vision designed within our own minds. Young persons (5-7years) have, more often, far more vivid imaginations than teenagers and adults within the same culture. Systematic conditioning doesn't usually set in until we begin to approach our teen years.

So, why did I not fall in love with Patricia in return? Perhaps I wasn't supposed to – by virtue of the fact that it didn't go that way. This teaches me that love cannot be prophesied or pre-empted, nor can it be forced. We either love someone or we don't. There is no middle ground. Sadly for Pat, she was heartbroken because I didn't have a passion for her.

My love for Hip-Hop and Soul had a backlash effect on me at that time. I was influenced into thinking and behaving in a certain way. I was more concerned about looking good – avoiding looking bad, being right – avoiding being wrong etc. One might say that the influences of music, as is propagated by the media, had me behaving in ways that were behind my 'better' judgement.

In truth, it was my own interpretation of the music and its contents that led me to think and act as I did, not the music itself. Certainly, it is not the intention of the founders of the Hip-Hop culture to propagate and encourage 'men-behaving-badly' scenarios. Not that I recognised these things at the time, but, in retrospect, I'm now able to evaluate my own cultural behavioural conditioning, whether influenced by the media or through my own volition.

I'm now able to see myself as exactly as I am, based upon many years of 'Personal Development' and 'Life-Coaching' training.

I became a graduate of the 'Landmark Forum,' which is an educational program delivered by LEC, (Landmark Education Corporation), which I wrote about in volume 1 of 'Urban Cries.' I also completed the Anthony Robbins' UPW, 'Unleash the Power Within' personal development seminar. The title ought to speak for itself at this point – but more on Mr Robbins later.

Through Landmark in particular, I was able to see, and realise, the genesis of my ways of thinking and, ways of being, from a very young age. I was able to understand my choices of partners at specific times of my life with great insight. During the Landmark Forum I was also presented with the possibility of recreating my life moment-to-moment, and therefore living the life I want to live. With the combined knowledge and insight I received from both training programs, I am now able to attain a complete view of my life – not simply in retrospect, but as an observer – to consciously be 'present' to each event as though it were someone else's. This is a very powerful position to be in, as I will explain in proceeding chapters.

Moreover, the two programs mentioned have had profound effects on my life in other ways. It is their tools and mental technologies that I wish to relay to you as you read through this work, which is in the context of Music culture. I wish to share with you, in essence, what's available to us, as far as true human potential is concerned.

Those who are familiar with my writings, will already know that I'm also affiliated to the teachings and programs of the NOI, (the Nation of Islam), and the UNNM, (the United Nuwaubian Nation of Moors). And of course, I will be sharing some of the tools and mental technologies of these in an educational manner, as it was for me on entering these schools. The intention here is to also present their doctrines with respect to the Blackman and Blackwoman connecting to the Creator, again within the context of Music culture.

Now... if you have ever been in a situation where you supposedly broke someone's heart, you may have asked yourself the question: "How may I un-break his/her heart?" It is very easy to just say: "What is done is done." Sometimes an apology, as sincere as you are with it, simply isn't enough. I certainly had this experience with Patricia, and later with others. I did not know how to un-break her heart, as much as I sincerely wanted her to move on and be happy with herself and her life.

But karma for me wasn't far round the corner. We will, on that thought, look at the 'Law of Intention and Karma' shortly.

> **Take responsibility for your own emotions.
> Become Present to them.
> Your emotions represent divine lessons,
> disguised as undesirable experiences.**

In the event of trying to apologise to an ex partner, who refuses to listen, for hurting his or her feelings, sometimes we have to bypass them on the third dimensional level and connect to their higher Self. By doing this, through prayer and meditation, we are able to give and receive grace, which is divine mercy. So teaches the 'Law of Grace and Mercy.'

The karmic heartbreaking scenario was reciprocated by way of my second, significant relationship.

Millie, another mentally strong girlfriend of mine, unlike Patricia, was not just in love with me, but on the flip-side wasn't prepared to put up with a guy who didn't know how to show a girl a good time. My income was non-existent, as I was still in my last year of school and so had no job. I didn't have many options in mind as to what to do to entertain a girl who was eager for laughs. Well here's the dilemma: for those who don't already know, I have a speech impediment, a stutter. As a result I was very quiet and somewhat shy around the girls. Patricia obviously didn't have a problem with this. It was like a protection mechanism for her – me not being brave enough to be chasing girls all the time, as my friends were. To her, my stutter would impede me from doing so.

But Millie made sure I knew that my boring her to death with lack of conversation was an issue to be reckoned with.

> **Embrace the fullness of a situation or experience. Align with all limitations. You will realise deep within that all is well.**

So, I guess the biggest lesson I learnt from Millie, was one of 'coming out of my self.' I had learnt the importance of being a little extrovert at times. God would often assign to us situations in which we have to vigorously step out of our 'comfort-zone' in order to sustain a relationship, or even to keep up appearances. This is regardless of the type of relationship – not just our love relationships.

Again, I didn't realise these things at the time – I was only able to see the reality of the experiences in retrospect, due to my training. I now understand that the limitations of life are what make us human. By aligning with the emotions of feeling constrained in self-expression, we align with Spirit, we align with the deepest part of being human: God. Here, we receive the lessons which prepare us for a divine blessing.

Millie was also passionate about Hip-Hop, like me. In fact, she was a rapper, and was very good at it. So we had an *urban* connection, at least. We would sometimes sit and listen to each other mimic Hip-Hop emcees and groups such as Big Daddy Kane, KRS One, Roxanne Shante, Public Enemy, Eric B. & Rakim and others. We could even relate to, to some extent, the lyrics of some of the more urban type Soul songs – this was where our more romantic times were enjoyed.

> **Remember the good experiences about your life.**
> **Positive memories will bring you moments of happiness, Joy and amusement**

In my later years (2004-2006), (bearing in mind my earlier introvert confrontations with Millie,) because of my personal development training, I knew how to break through the emotional bondage of those once limiting mental states. Yes, stuttering, as well as quietness, and even extroversion and flamboyance, on the contrary, are governed by specific mental states. These mental states can conjure up specific emotions which go on to sustain the conditions that inhibit us, but only if we allow these states of mind to persist.

By aligning with negative emotional energy, you are able to realise the lessons there to be learned. Once you acknowledge and thank the Angelic Ones for allowing you the opportunity to receive the lesson, you are then ready for the blessings of transformation and ascension.

As a student/teacher of the esoteric, I have had the opportunity to lecture before classes on various subjects including the origin of religion, Afrokhan culture, food and diet, government conspiracies, ancient and modern spirituality, and more. This advance in my abilities had been a 'no-way-how-say' thought in my teenage years.

So, if you, my dear reader, have ever felt inhibited, or are one who feels limited in self-expression, then stay with me on this for a chapter or two.

Here is the deal. With the 'Unleash the Power Within' seminar, lead by Tony Robbins, I acquired some very simple but powerful tools, which enable people to change their mental states virtually at the snap of a finger. Thus, by consciously selecting or choosing specific mental states, one is able to produce desired emotions at will, by way of our thoughts, and also by using the appropriate physical posture.

The question is why is this type of information coming out at this time? The esoteric establishments of the world have kept these doctrines sacred and secret for hundreds of years. So why now?

Why did the powerful technology of Landmark come forth to the people? Why did the powerful technologies of Tony Robbins become accessible? Consider, these are only two of such mental-technology training programs. Others include Scientology, NLP, Cold and Warm Reading and more.

Looking back over the last twenty-five years or so, the Hip-Hop culture has been through many transitions. Its founders, people like Afrika Bambaata, Kool Hercs, Grandmaster Flash, Kurtis Blow and the like, used the emceeing aspects of the movement to propagate a very powerful message to the Black Community, and indeed to anyone else who would listen. These messages, if I may view them in an unintended context, were nature's ways of preparing Black folks of America, and the western world in general, for an awakening – to be raptured into fourth-dimensional awareness.

So it is my understanding that Black organisations such as the Nation of Islam and the United Nuwaubian Nation of Moors also propagate similar doctrines in order to prepare devotees for fourth-dimensional awareness – an esoterical prospective way of connecting to God.

⌀

Connecting with God

Personally speaking, my combined life experiences have unexpectedly rewarded me with a connection to my Creator. There have been many, very different scenarios, which I was able to align with, to receive divine lessons and to strengthen my connection to my Creator. I wish to share with you how I have been able to achieve higher states of awareness, through my more significant relationships with women.

Life is a school, beloved, the earth plane is a classroom, and, our various experiences are the subjects, the lessons, that each and every one of us is supposed to learn. Each individual is a vessel of the Creator, God. Through our interacting with one another, we interact with God. Through our relationships, particularly the significant loved ones, we intimately connect with the Creator, God.

Remember the title of this work:

'A Blackman's connection to God through the Blackwoman.'

This places the man aspect of nature as a corresponder. That is to say, through man, woman is able to make a connection to God. But paradoxically, man himself cannot make that connection fully, without woman. In other words, a constant flow of energy, the love vibration in this instance, cannot occur unless the circuit is complete. Consider the diagram below:

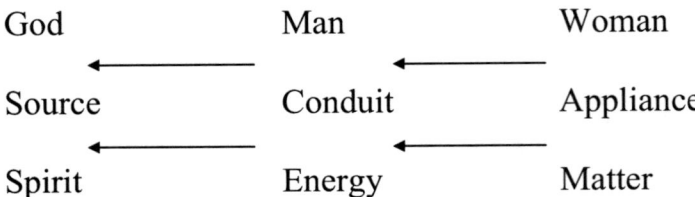

Symbolically, God represents the source of our household electrical supply – Woman represents the appliance to be utilised. Man therefore represents the conduit, or the electrical cable. So as can easily be seen, the three have to be connected in order for a constant flow of energy to occur – the love vibration. Furthermore, man is sky-bound, or celestial in nature, and, woman is terrestrial. We can observe this biblically, where man is created in the image of God, (metaphorically meaning the imagination of God,) which from our perspectives would be of Spirit, or at least celestial. We then have a physical manifestation of man, from which woman is symbolically drawn from his rib (meaning, DNA from his bone marrow) and thus manifested.

This creates an anchoring connection of mankind to the earth plane through the female, and likewise figuratively speaking an anchoring of mankind to the spiritual plane through the male.

Scientifically speaking this also proves to be a correct analysis. The male having a centrifugal force about his nature, which is a force pushing upwards connects him to the celestial – Spirit. And the female, having a centripetal force about her nature, which is a force pushing downwards connects her to the terrestrial – Matter. Therefore, in combination, and with perfect harmony, we have a constant flow of the love vibration.

A Blackman's Connection to God through the Blackwoman

It is through woman then, that man makes his connection to the Earth, to matter. This is with respect to Subjective—Objective polarity, or respectively, Heaven—Earth polarity. Therefore, it is through man that woman makes her connection to Heaven, Spirit, and God. It is within this context that the male, culturally speaking, is usually preferred or accepted to be the Pope, the Rabbis, the Imam, the Minister, Pastor, Teacher and Preacher etc.

However, matrilineal rulership throughout the ancient world was a stance taken from within an entirely different context, as we shall see in Chapter 4.

It was upon my entering the doors of the 'Nation of Islam,' that I first heard of the significance of the Blackwoman, and her connection to God through the Blackman. At first, I thought this was just some Islamic male chauvinist's ego, in woman-belittling mode. But, the scientific understanding, as shown above, came to me when I learnt of Dr York and his teachings. The statement was somewhat re-worded like this: the Female acquires her Subjective connection through the Male, whilst the Male acquires his Objective connection through the Female. Looking at it this way changes the meaning drastically.

However:

> "A Nation can rise no higher than its Woman"
>
> Farrakhan

Minister Farrakhan, leader of the NOI, had also given a speech entitled, *'A Nation can rise no higher than its Woman,'* in which he spoke to women only and in which, for me, a profound sense of clarity was delivered.

Prior to my acquiring such knowledge, however, I had gone through some more very significant relationships and experiences, including those of Hazel and Angie. This eventful period of my life was to change everything forever.

Hazel and I had met at a friend's house in Peckham, London. I was about sixteen to seventeen at the time. We, the group of friends at the house, were patriots of the Hip-Hop and RnB culture. The term bling-bling hadn't existed yet, but for sure, the mentality to show and tell was eminent. Read on...

Ch.2

The Hip-Hop & RnB Culture
Show and tell!

Ever fell victim to 'love at first sight'? Need I say more then?

Guys, have you ever ended up wearing someone else's jacket? If you have, then you already know what I'm about to say. I found out through experience what is meant by 'wearing another man's jacket.' It means, taking on a relationship with a pregnant woman, whose child is not yours, but with you intending to raise the child as your own. And, that is exactly what I did with Hazel.

Well, not quite. When we met she wasn't already pregnant. No, that would have been too easy.

> Responsibility is a grace you give yourself.
> You cannot impose it on another.
> Show unconditional desire to be responsible,
> and the Universe will empower you ten-fold.

So you've guessed it! This is where I encountered my first *'having an affair,'* experience. I was, but not to my knowledge, having a relationship with a woman who had some 'unfinished business'. She broke the news to me about what had been going on with her ex-partner. There were thoughts of the possibility of being pregnant. I was angry, I was mad, and I lashed out.

We had been split up for several weeks or so before we finally talked. We spoke of the possibility of going ahead with her having the child and us raising it as ours. Needless to say, Hazel did fall in love with me, eventually. It was only through our love for each other that we were able to arrive at such contingencies.

This was the biggest responsibility I had ever taken on, to date. But I wasn't empowered to deal with it appropriately. I did it for all the wrong reasons, although I was convinced, within myself, that I was doing a good thing.

No one was to know about this, not even the real father. Some friend I was, huh. Yep, you've guessed it again. The baby's father and I were associates, so I wasn't in a hurry to forgive and forget.

> ## Give and receive Grace,
> ## It is the Divine Mercy that sets people Free.
> Diana Cooper

Forgiveness, a faculty of Grace, is a very powerful force indeed. But I hadn't realised the importance of this life faculty until years later. In relation to this, we will look at the 'Seven Laws of Human Inter-relationship' in a few pages ahead. The appendix section of the book will also shed a little more light on these spiritual principles.

I also found it at the time very difficult to forgive Hazel, although I was willing to move forward as daddy.

Consequently, I couldn't help myself falling into a two-timing scenario myself.

Remember… you become what you resist, or, you become that which you dislike or hate. This happens since the subconscious mind does not understand the difference between positive and negative thoughts. It simply works to manifest that which we focus on.

Actually, Hazel and I split up several times during the pregnancy, due to my constantly arguing with her, making her bad, and making her wrong. Have you ever heard the saying, *'there is a thin line between love and hate?'* I loved and hated her at the same time.

Now, Angie, a friend of a friend, was to enter the scenario in such a way that greatly amplified the drama of the situation. We met during one of those times when Hazel and I were separated (which was usually no more than two-three days, one week at the most). Angie became pregnant with my first child – or was that the case? I mean, everyone believed that Hazel and I were having a baby which was soon due.

What a predicament! Words cannot really describe what this felt like for me. Not having the guts to speak to Patricia about my true feelings was one thing, but this? How was I going to explain to Hazel what I had done? I did in fact reveal the situation to Angie, and she took it well at the time, I think…

Do you want to hear some more drama? The real father of Hazel's baby, my so-called friend, was no fool. He knew exactly what was happening, and quite rightly confronted her. However, this pissed me right off, as you can imagine. It was like tit-for-tat, our pissing each other off.

By the time I had found the energy and courage to tell Hazel the truth, he had already taken his stance to let us know that he was here to stay – as the baby's father.

> **The Truth shall set you free.**
>
> Christ Jesus

By taking on the responsibility of his child, without his permission, and indeed without the permission of the Angelic Ones, not to mention that I also didn't ask the unborn baby for permission to be its father, I was trapped in fear of embarrassment and guilt. I was not free.

With all the above in mind, my biggest challenge was in deciding what to do with regard to letting my friends know the unbearable truth. Of course, I had also to make a decision between the two ladies.

Show and tell? Remember, it's all about looking good, avoiding looking bad, being right, avoiding being wrong, etc. Did I actually tell my friends the truth? Nope. Not even my family (my mother), at least not for many years. The payoff was that I had to be seen as 'being the man,' in the eyes of my friends. I couldn't afford to taint my image of looking good, and I had to appear justified and so on.

My life was to take another twist when I was initiated into the philosophy of AfroCentricity. I was nineteen years old when I first heard about the legacy of the Black man and woman. I was taught about the aesthetics, the beauty of being Black, of being *African*, and of being the original humans of earth. (I later defined my own spelling of the word as **Afrokhan**, see Appendix H). This is when I was introduced to the likes of Minister Louis Farrakhan, Malcolm X, Marcus Garvey, Martin Luther King Jr and many others. Their messages to me at the time were of power – Black power. It was around this time when I began to realise what the real Hip-Hop Culture was about.

☼

<u>The Aesthetics of Hip-Hop</u>
Oh, by the way, in case you were wondering what happened with my dilemma, I had ended up with Angie – but only for about one year. Hazel and I, although we were at each other's throats for obvious reasons, we were to become very good friends in the years ahead. To contrast with this I later became Angie's enemy! We will return to this in Part 3.

A question is – what is it that drives us to have 'love' affairs? Some psychologists argue that for some people, the possession of a simple desire to be with someone that they cannot have, amplifies the sexual drive and increases the tension and anxiety of the desire. Sexologist, Dr. Jack Morin, came up with what he calls the 'Erotic Equation,' which is: Attraction plus Obstacle = Erotic Charge. In other words, a basic sexual attraction between two people can become magnified if some opposing, usually forbidden, element is present.[1]

Within all communities we have situations of cheating husbands and wives. Within the original Hip-Hop culture, there were Rappers that spoke out of these realities.

Hip-Hop was empowering for me. For it presented a wake up call doctrine within which many were called but few chose to listen. I actually wanted to become an emcee myself. I had a few friends who also had the same ambition and in a short time we had formed ourselves a group. The trouble was, we were all wanna-bees, including our supposed producer. As much as we loved music and wanted to produce music, we were not really cut out for it. The group split up eventually, this was not surprising.

Later on the wanna-be producer gave me a phone call regarding doing a backing Rap for a woman who wanted to remix version of a song she had previously recorded. The song was called 'Reality.' I felt this was gonna be a great opportunity for me, but it wasn't the opportunity I was expecting.

Gill, the singer, was thirty years old, I was twenty, but our connection was one of lust more than anything else.

○

It was a unique experience for me at the time – to be with a much older woman. The 'Law of Projection and Attraction' was loud and clear in this scenario. In retrospect, again.

For more clarity, here is a quick synopsis of the 'Seven Laws of Human Inter-relationship':

> *Law-1*   The Law of One and Interconnectedness
> This affirms that there can be no separation from the Creator; therefore, there is no separation between man and the *persons*, *places* and *things* of his life.

Law-2   The Law of Intention and Karma
This affirms that, as a man thinks, intends and does – his deeds will eventually come right back to him in exactly the same proportion as he gave them out.

Law-3   The Law of Projection and Attraction
This affirms that what we project in energy comes right back to us in the form of *persons*, *places* or *things*. For instance, one may attract the conditions of poverty because he sends out that kind of energy in terms of negative thoughts of being poor. He therefore finds himself constantly surrounded with undesirable mediocre circumstances.

Law-4   The Law of Grace and Mercy
This affirms that unconditional forgiveness and compassion dissolves karma and reaps blessings.

Law-5   The Law of Responsibility and Godliness
This affirms that by man taking responsibility for his thoughts, intentions and actions, he can master the affairs of his life. He is therefore able to respond to the experiences of his life appropriately, hence, response-ability.

Law-6   The Law of Integrity and Manifestation
This affirms that *'As a man thinketh in his heart, so is he.'* Integrity is the key to manifestation. Manifestation is confirmation of Integrity. Whatever we believe to be a possibility we can manifest. The intensity of how we visualise that possibility strengthens the integrity of the intention for manifestation. Integrity and Manifestation brings into reality a preconceived idea, regardless of circumstances.

<u>*Law*-7</u>   <u>The Law of Unconditional Love</u>
This affirms that True Love is to love unconditionally – without any objective, reason or intention. Unconditional love for 'All that Is,' raises awareness of Self up to higher realms of be*ing* in which one aligns with the Angelic Ones – the Helpers of the Creator.

◯

So why was I attracted to an older woman, and why was she attracted to me? The only obvious thing we had in common, practically speaking, was our desire to create and produce music.

By studying the 'Law of Projection and Attraction,' we can see that the majority of what a person projects, in terms of energy, happens subconsciously. He is not even aware of it. As a consequence, much of what he attracts is also through subconscious magnetism.

Our soul is on a journey. Not just through the physical life we are currently experiencing, but also a celestial journey – a journey that brings us to this great school of Self-realisation: Earth. Some of the experiences of the soul are necessary for it to ascend. These experiences are designed to help unburden the soul of negative energy acquired from past lives. Other experiences are desired if the soul has never had those experiences in past incarnations.

The reality is that we choose to manifest on Earth at this time. We petitioned the Angelic Ones, for us to incarnate at this time in order to learn specific lessons – perhaps to re-sit previously failed tests or to take on new experiences. This means that we actually chose our parents, our families, and the environment in which to be born and raised – we chose everything. Our being here is not an accident, we have a self-imposed mandate.

However, in this particular era, those of us present on earth are blessed with a remarkable responsibility. This is to unburden our souls of the negative energy that it has incurred over many lifetimes. We are blessed to be present at this time, as there are a large number of avatars on earth today. These are spiritual guides that are divinely ordained to aid in the ascension of humanity.

Planet Earth, as a whole has petitioned its Creator to move towards fourth and fifth dimensional realms. The purpose of this is to unburden itself of negative energy. To make the shift, earth's constituents' (men, animals and all life forms), all souls <u>must</u> be unburdened too.

This is where the aesthetics of the Hip-Hop culture blows its trumpet.

Gill and I were called together through music, through Hip-Hop. The title of the song, had it been completed and released was intended to be: 'Reality.' Was this a coincidence? I think not.

The time is Now.

The aesthetics of a culture is its beauty and its splendour. The beauty of the Hip-Hop culture is its propagation of spiritual enlightenment – one of raising awareness, confidence, integrity, responsibility, grace, forgiveness and prosperity. The culture also promotes coalitions for multi-cultural united economics, business relations, and transformative education for all peoples. This is the thesis and argument of Volume 1 of 'Urban Cries' – *'Communicating with God through Music & Performing Arts, &, The Implications of the Hip-Hop Culture.'*

The rhetorical aesthetics of Hip-Hop has brought us a range of 'wake-up call' philosophies, which, one might say, has been hugely successful. But, the time has now arrived for us to take these principles or philosophies more seriously. This means we ought to be able to understand that third dimensional *laws* are simply guidelines that are set up by men as a means to uphold specific fourth dimensional *principles*. These men are usually guided by the Angelic Ones and they are called ascended masters, avatars, channels, and, at least sixteen of such men have been called *Christ* according to the book, *'The World's Sixteen Crucified Saviours,'* by Kersey Graves.

Man-made laws, (whether governmental, or divinely influenced,) will always change according to the level of consciousness of a people, and their time zone but spiritual principles are sound, they never change. This is regardless also of the time zone. So, although we are entertaining 'The Seven Laws of Human Inter-relationship' here, behind them we are actually acknowledging profound fourth dimensional principles. This is something I would like you to understand.

○

The deepest part of being Human
The deepest part of being human is realised through our acknowledgement of the very laws and principles that govern human behaviour. These realisations, once put into practice, reward us with the keys to the gates of heaven.

Heaven is not just a place where the righteous go when they die, nor is it so for the unrighteous to go to hell. Heaven is created from within, just as hell is also created from within. Through our childhood programming, right up to exactly where we are now, we have been creating our own reality. How we respond to that reality in turn determines whether or not we live in heaven, or hell.

The deepest part of being human, as reiterated by KRS One, is being God – Spirit. It is realising your part or purpose within the bigger scheme of the Universe, of God.

Through proper prayer and proper meditation we discover our deepest potentials; we discover our true purpose. We are little angels of the Creator here on earth – we are Its children.

Prayer defined is simply to communicate with the divine, within. Other than through prayer, you can communicate with the divine in many other ways, including through music, poetry, artistry (like pottery or painting), chanting Aum or counting inhales and exhales of deep breaths. Repetitive mantras, affirmations and supplications are also means of prayer. Volume 1 of 'Urban Cries' emphasises how God and Man interrelate through the medium of music; man's creativity in his music no doubt comes from his Creator, and, God's messages of inspiration comes to us through divinely inspired music. This is not only true of Hip-Hop culture; it is true for all musically orientated cultures.

> **Prayer is communication with your Creator.**
> **But, you must take the time to listen to**
> **what He has to say in response,**
> **and then express gratitude.**

Meditation on the other hand, is to listen to the Divine. You can also listen to the Divine in a number of other ways. Meditation is achieved through trance, daydreaming, and also through artistic activities. Meditation works, and is achieved for different people in different ways.

By becoming preoccupied with a task, you can enter the Divine vibration in which you receive inspirations and answers that aid in the dissolving of undesirables in your life. You can also meditate by intimately listening to the sound of the wind, the sound of water splashing by a river's bank, or even by listening to rainfall. You can also meditate by aligning with beautiful scents, whether it is the smell of aroma oils, incense, or the smell of food being prepared. You can also meditate by visually focusing on some detail of an object, such as a candle's flame, or a leaf sticking out the top of an orange or apple. Taste, is also an avenue that leads to meditation. This can be achieved when counting the chews of a specific fruit or vegetable and aligning with its taste, or, by focusing on the memory of that delicious taste. Finally by sense of touch, and with the eyes closed, you can achieve meditation by aligning with the texture of something held, such as an orange's skin.

So it can be seen that a meditative state can be reached through the use of the five senses. 'Meditation' and 'Prayer' have been largely misunderstood by the masses of western society. Prayer is not about begging God for something, or to appease Him when in religious congregations: to show and tell.

God does not answer our prayers, in terms of saying *yes*, if we are not humble enough to receive our lessons. Think about this. Why would you feel the need to pray and ask for help with a seemingly impossible situation? The situation itself may present an opportunity for you to learn a certain lesson or lessons. If you are too quick to ask God for help in getting you out of your predicament, without consciously receiving the lesson therein, He will reply, '*No!*'

However, whenever we receive our lessons with humility, by spiritual law we also receive grace and forgiveness. The Angelic Ones will then guide us into our receiving the answers.

Solutions to problems can come to us through meditation, a sudden thought, through feeling, or a gesture from someone else. If you consider examples from your own experience, is this not true?

☥

As we approach Part 2, I must remind you that chapters 3-7 encompass an expanded-upon chapter taken from my book *'The Mystical and Magical Paths of Self and not-self,'* Vol 2. I say this because the wording of the following information is of a sophisticated nature. It was originally intended for fourth dimensional thinkers. It takes an esoteric standpoint. You will come across statements and ideologies that may not sit right with your current beliefs.

This need not be a problem; the deepest part of one's being – that which is in contact with the Angelic Ones, will guide your intuition.

☥

When I was about twenty-two years old I met Marian, with whom I was to have my next significant relationship, after Gill.

She had the kind of upbringing that I found to be very unusual, I had not met this before. She and her older sister had been fostered and so raised by a white family. Their Ghanaian parents had deliberately given them up for fostering, for reasons that I could not agree with or understand at the time. In retrospect, I can see why Marian had a difficult time trusting anybody who ever got close to her, men in particular.

This was a very challenging relationship for both of us, particularly because I already had a child with someone else, whom I would always be in contact with. We loved each other, no doubt, but we argued more than anything else. We just couldn't seem to get along. I was annoyed with her for not understanding why she would not trust me. It was through Marian then, that I really got to understand that there is a big issue amongst Black couples when it comes to trust, loyalty and faithfulness.

However, I thank the Angelic Ones for allowing us to spend more than two years of our lives together. We learned some very significant lessons about ourselves and about life.

¤

A Blackman's Connection to God through the Blackwoman

Part_2

The Science of Love in the Making
—————— Revised ——————

> The material world as we perceive it is but a manifestation of *energy* that is expressed in different forms; either as electrical, radioactive or magnetic currents – which are the product of the tearing energy coming from the Light of God, (the Ain-Soph-Aur of the Kaballion.) That, which is perceived as the gross physical body of the Oriental, the Asian and the Caucasian, is of the gross astral light, and is but the cohesion of electrical and radioactive energies having a physical experience. The Afrokhan's gross physical body is of the Divine Astral Light, and, materialises as the cohesion of electrical and magnetic forces. We experience electrochemical synaptic impulses within the nervous system, which we translate as e-motions of joy and pain, love and hate etc. And ultimately we experience 'love making,' as the highest and most powerful form of physical e-motion.
>
> Nebu Ka Ma'at
MMSN Vol.2

Ch.3

Impulsive behaviour

Impulsive behaviour simply means to act on impulse, or, to act on sudden urges. It also means to act or react to our emotions or to have impetuous emotional responses without the intervention of logical thoughts. This is the derived expression of Western society, as it propagates its interpretation of what love and sexuality means through different elements of the media.

However, the purpose of Part_2: 'The Science of Love in the Making,' is to give the reader an understanding of why and how we fall in and out love, and, why we make Love, and to understand the magical sciences of ritualistic intercourse and its positive and negative implications. We must grow to understand the power of intercourse as well as the negative impacts that can be inflicted upon the physical body if we misuse it.

Intercourse can indeed be a wonderful experience, especially when it is done with someone we truly love. However, most of us tend to have sexual intercourse just for the sheer enjoyment of it. This is purely a mechanical feat. It is like a two-handled slot machine with two operators trying to get a jackpot at the same time.

Surely this cannot be what sex is all about!

Sexual Energy

Sexual energy, – or the energy that is transferred during the act of intercourse is the highest form of energy that the human body can impart or absorb. For us to understand these energy transferences it is imperative that we have an understanding of energy in general. Everything within our universe is based upon energy, and as a microcosm of the cosmos, human beings are an amalgamation of energy also.

All physical matter is a coagulation of units of force expressed as energy, and thus energy is required for the maintenance of all physical manifestations – all of which are controlled and directed by the Universal Mind; the Subjective Conscience of the Self. Energy and Spirit are one and the same, and matter, is a physical manifestation of Spirit – or Spirit in its lowest form of vibration.

Humans are created and are thus born with a certain amount of energy, called *Chi* energy or *Sekhem* or *Prana*.[A] This original substantial energy cannot be replaced once it has been used up, but it can be replenished by way of our diet, and our breathing, and is also dependent on a sound state of mind. The amount of energy or quality of energy we ingest or expel is largely determined by our mental state of be*ing*.

We think our selves into who and what we become, which is then enhanced by the foods we eat and the quality of air we breathe. This also means we think our selves into our own demise due to the lack of awareness of whom and what we are – due to the lack of Conscience and Divine Astral awareness. We create our 'somatic body'[B] based upon the

---

[A] The Orientals know this vital life force as Chi, it is known as Sekhem in ancient Khemet, and as Prana to the Hindus.

[B] The somatic body is created and grown by the mental programming of the soma cells, where these cells are constantly being reproduced, as opposed to our germ cells that never die. Somatic programming has become one of the fundamental means of

conditioning of the latter. We are conditioned to believe that we can only live for a certain amount of years, and so this subconsciously programs the brain to create a somatic body with a limited life span.

Sexual energy, if understood and used correctly is one of many stepping-stones toward immorality. This is because of the unlimited amount of spiritual energy that can be attained by way of intercourse.

There is an old saying:

> 'The making of man and woman, is like the making of heaven and earth.'

Humans have long forgotten this aphorism. It is an axiom that embodies the truth that heaven and earth i.e. stars and planets can live for aeons upon aeons of time. In ancient Afrokhan and Asiatic cultures this axiom was clearly understood and people led a way of life that was focused on developing their ability to harness and store Chi energy. One of these methods was to master the use of Sexual Energy and Force.

The purpose of intercourse is to enable the participants to reach higher states of awareness and consciousness. It should not be intended just to reach ejaculation or to have an ecstatic orgasm! In fact, ejaculation and orgasm are two completely different biological functions. In the male, ejaculation is but a physiological function that is hardwired into the brain for the sole purpose of procreation when the penis is stimulated through intercourse or otherwise.

---

systematic mind control, because these cells can be conditioned to mentally produce a body that will be in line with the enforced mental state.

Ejaculation within intercourse should therefore only happen if the intention of both parties is to have a child – to procreate in correspondence with the divine order.

The amount of Sekhem or Chi energy that is used up during every ejaculation is equivalent to an unfit male doing a 20-mile run within a 5-10min slot! This is devastating to the body. Hence, professional athletes are always being advised by their coach to refrain from sexual activities for at least three days before they perform.

> *'Abstaining from ejaculation for 90 days can develop sexual potency, as it takes 90 days to fully develop sperm. Unused fully developed sperm is then dissipated and spread throughout the body as an energy source. Remember... each time the male ejaculates he is using up his life essence – Chi – Sekhem. A very Yang-male, with fully developed sperm can ejaculate up to 777,777,777 sperm in one go.'*[2]
>
> Paraphrased from Dr Malachi

> *"On the average the male may ejaculate up to 5,000 times within his lifetime or ejaculate 5 gallons of sperm in total."*[3]
>
> Wayne Chandler

Sexual Mantras

A mantra is a vocally produced tone or series of tones in the form of a chant or chants, which resonate within the body to invoke specific energies. During the act of intercourse we may fall into an automatic mantra without realising it. The moans or groans that we experience are the result of our neurological system corresponding with the brain – informing it that climax is on the way.

The moans are automatically produced as forms of mantras to incite our spiritual centres to open up thereby allowing the divine aspect of the entity to be incarnated to enter. If moans or groans are not produced, one will find oneself automatically breathing deeply.

Breathing deeply is a very convenient and powerful way of aligning all of our spiritual centres – such as the chakras. (See appendix for further information on the chakras). Breathing deeply also powerfully helps to revitalise the body in totality. Mantras and chants, when done intentionally and consciously should be performed with specific breath taking exercises.

Sexual intercourse should therefore be treated as a sacred ritual.

☿

During coitus, or just before ejaculation, the <u>spirit of the semen</u> follows the path of the **Khundalini**,[A] by rising up along the spinal column passing all major Chakra points until it reaches the *medulla oblongata*, the brain stem. Here, the 'spark of life' occurs – the 'Big Bang' of Sekhem/Chi – the entity to be incarnated enters via the pineal gland. It then marries with the semen at the junction of the brain stem and the spinal column. Here, the spirit of the semen is synergized with the spirit of the incarnated being, consciousness. The spiritual entity then travels back down the spinal column in a rush, marries with the actual semen, the liquid form, which

---

[A] The word Khundalini is sometimes translated as the sleeping serpent, where the serpent is symbolic of healing and transformation.

now becomes sperm and ejaculates through the phallus on its way to seek fertilisation of the female ovum.

So the act of coitus, coupled with correct conscious breathing and linked to automatic mantras is but a spiritual science performed on the physical level, but with psycho-spiritual correspondences.

This connects us to higher vibratory planes of existence and experience. At this level of spiritual initiation one can *choose* to bring a new life into the world by way of ejaculation, or may otherwise choose to simply enjoy the experience which ends with full rejuvenation of the body, without actual ejaculation.

☿

The raising of the Khundalini during intercourse is extremely powerful, if we understand how to harness and use the available energy. Each Chakra along the spinal column represents one of the seven planes of existence and experience. The seven major chakras are shown overleaf, table 1.

Generally, the Khundalini energy lays dormant within the Root Chakra, as most of earth's humans are only consciously in tune with the plane of physical manifestation. As the Khundalini energy rises, whether through meditation, chanting, breathing or coitus, one becomes consciously attuned to the corresponding planes. Understand that there are specific techniques of meditation, chants, breaths and intercourse that enable us to tune in and experience these higher states of awareness.

Table 1: the 7Chakras and corresponding Planes

Chakra	Plane of manifestation
Crown Chakra	Bosom of God
Brow Chakra	Plane of Divine Reality
Throat Chakra	Plane of Divine Truth
Heart Chakra	Plane of Mind
Solar Plexus Chakra	Plane of Spiritual Animation
Spleenic Chakra	Plane of Spiritual Force
Root Chakra	Plane of Physical Manifestation

Ch.4

Love in Creational Myths

The Divinity of Love has to be at the root of the conception of the universe and of God's Creations. Without Divine Love, manifestation will not happen, because Divine Love is the basis of Subjective Integrity. Divine Love is the ultimate healer also, projected by the Divine Astral Light.

The raising of the Khundalini brings us back in tune with the Creator, Conscience and Love, which by default affords us youthfulness and vitality in the moment. This means that one who is on the mystical path ought to live life in meditation – meaning we must consciously travel, talk, eat, and sleep etc., in meditation.

> We often hear the 'truth' that God created the world out of Love.

This type of Love is not to be confused with desires to have a *thing* or to have an *experience*. This is Love beyond mental description – a Presence that is achieved once we escape the boundaries of time and polarity consciousness – a Presence coupled with Divine Peace and Joy. This Presence of be*ing* rewards us with the ultimate gift of unlimited creativity and infinite potential. It is the reality of being 'Present in the Now.'

Yin and Yang

The source of our yin and yang aspects is derived directly out of Love. In the 3 dimensional world of manifestation, these aspects represent our duality concepts of male and female, masculine and feminine or positive and negative, centrifugal and centripetal forces etc., all of which are objective. The source of Love is therefore Subjective and is perfectly and completely united. The Subjective Mind unites all of Creation as one Created phenomenon, as one complete experience. Our interpretation of the objective manifestation of the world gives rise to the illusion of space/time/separation etc.

As we manifest into the world of duality and of low vibratory rates, we loose our perception (due to amnesia, from the shock and trauma at birth) of the interconnectedness of all *things*. We also forget that we have a higher aspect to our be*ing*, referred to as our twin flame or twin Soul. This higher aspect usually resides in the 4th dimension although it can be experiencing ever higher dimensions simultaneously.

However, the DNA is encoded in such a way that we periodically remember that there is something missing from our lives. The Astral Light triggers us involuntarily through DNA excitement since it holds all the information and memory of our entire existence.

This memory jogger may also be triggered, by watching movies like Star Trek or Babylon 5, or by listening to a spiritual sermon, or even by reading self-empowerment books such as this one. But due to our own ignorance, that which constrains us, we tend to seek out this twin soul in our so-called love relationships.

We set out on an earthly mission to find our soul mate. And assuming that we have 'found' her/him, ultimately the act of coitus or 'love making' gives us the experience of uniting with our 'soul mate' on a higher level. This is not to say that this is wrong, but to understand that intercourse, is a method that two people <u>standing in love</u> together can use as a vehicle to help each other connect with their own twin soul or to the Higher Self – not with each other!

This is the illusion of 3rd dimension and egoic conditioning. The ego-self has a tendency to obscure us from connecting to the Higher Self, so it tricks us into believing that we can find true Love, Peace and Joy in other than God. Yes, we do experience these 3 paradigms within our more serious relationships, but only as reflections of the real deal… in fact, that is the very nature of the ego – to give us reflections of Reality, which are in fact reflections of our inner being.

The ancient Khemetic mystery system taught its neophytes about the duality concepts of 3rd dimensional living. This was expressed by way of the anthropomorphic attributes of the Creator, (NTR,) as the deities Shu and Tefnut. In this context, Shu represents the yang (masculine) and Tefnut represents the yin (feminine). But Shu also expresses the yin within his yang nature, and likewise Tefnut expresses the yang within her yin nature. So, even though they are separated by way of duality consciousness, both are still complete within and of themselves – by way of their intimate connection with their own twin flame or soul – with God.

Ancient myths and legends are often sexually explicit in their narration of bi-sexual creative forces, such as the accounts of Aphrodite and Venus.

♀

Aphrodite and Venus

The planet Venus, the emblem of love and emotion, is the planet so attributed by the magical philosophers. Likewise the colour green, which traditionally belongs to Aphrodite, is peculiarly connected with growth, harvest and agriculture.

During the Neolithic times (the so-called later stone-age periods) the notion of a Goddess or of a woman as ruler of an entire tribe, people or nation was commonplace. This is especially so amongst the Sumerian and later the Babylonian, Anatolian and Canaan cultures of that era and indeed prior. There is a common theme, or concept, of a worshipped female deity, who is always portrayed with a young husband or lover. Some folklore presents their goddess as having sexual relations with her son or younger brother (obviously symbolic). We get reflections of this concept within the Greek legends of Aphrodite and Adonis, who were even known as Cybele and Attis in pre-Christian Rome.

Charles Seltman wrote, in 1952, of a highly developed culture of Crete, whose beginnings predate biblical times by many centuries. He states that, in Crete, matriarchy was the way of life. He discussed the sexual freedom of women, matrilineal descent, and the role of a *King*, pointing out the high status of women in and around the land in which the Goddess appears to have been the very core of existence. Men became *King* only by way of a formal marriage, and, his successor would be the man who married his daughter, not his son. In other words the women would choose who would become king.

In the upper Palaeolithic societies (the so-called early stone age periods) in which the mother may have been regarded as the sole parent of the family, ancestor worship was apparently the basis of sacred ritual, and, the means for ancestral reverence were generally carried out through matrilineal agents. This is because the concept of a Creator in the clan's image was female.

Images of goddesses of these Palaeolithic times, as far back as 25,000BCE, were called Venus figures, made of stones, bones and clay. The legendary Greek Goddess Aphrodite is also known as Venus in early Rome, as Astarte in Phoenicia, and as Ishtar in Babylonia.[4] She is said to be either the daughter of Zeus, or, she sprung from the foam of the seas. She is also said to be the mother of Eros, the Greek boy-god of love, identified with the Roman Cupid.

Now, the set of stories surrounding Aphrodite and Venus is based upon the idea that these pseudo Goddesses symbolise subliminal sexual aphrodisiacs. The Goddess is also portrayed as the notoriously unfaithful wife of Hephaestus, the God of fire.

What, you may ask, does all this have to do with True Love? I would say nothing. The majority of myths and folklore that we find concerning Love in Creation is either Hindi and Oriental or, Greek and Roman. Afrokhan cosmologies tend to deal more with balancing principles or, union of yin and yang forces etc., as opposed to aphrodisiac-base stories. One Hindu commentary talks of how the Creator Brahma was in a lovers embrace with his consort for what seemed like eternity before eventually ejaculating thus producing the first human beings.

Love & Sex in the Sumerian epics

I quote from the book of Genesis just as a reminder of where we find the apparently first acts relating to love and sex.

> *"And the eyes of them both were opened, and they knew that they were naked; and they sewed fig leaves together, and made themselves aprons."*
>
> Gen 3v8

And then in chapter 4 we have:

> *"And Adam knew his wife; and she conceived, and bare Cain, and said, I have gotten a man from the Lord."*
>
> Gen 4v1

In his book *'The Twelfth Planet,'* Zecharia Sitchin elaborates on these quotes and writes:

> *'They were, we are to understand, at some lesser stage of human development than that of fully developed humans: Not only were they naked, they were unaware of the implications of such nakedness.*
>
> *Further examination of the biblical tale suggests that its theme is Man's acquisition of some sexual powers. The "knowing" that was held back from Man was not some scientific information but something with the male and female sex; for no sooner had Man and his mate acquired the "knowing" than "they knew they were naked" and covered their sex organs.'*[5]
>
> Zecharia Sitchin

Throughout the Old Testament the term *'to know,'* is used to denote sexual intercourse, mostly between a man and his spouse for the purpose of having children. The quote informs the reader of the first act of sexual intercourse between the so-called Adam and Eve, the first man and woman. I do not put too fine a point on the fact that the consummation was not preceded by a formal agreement or wedding ceremony! Sitchin also extensively writes about the fact that the Genesis account is but a summary of ancient Babylonian and Sumerian texts, of which he spares no unturned stones in his book, *'Genesis Revisited.'* He says, *"the Mesopotamian texts speak freely and eloquently of sex and lovemaking among the gods"* – that is, the Anunnaqi.

There are texts that describe in detail, intimacy and tenderness among the gods. Some texts describe violent lovemaking also, such as, the raping of Ninlil by the god Enlil.

Other texts describe how the gods frequently indulged in sexual activity with their unofficial concubines, with their sisters and daughters, and even with their grand daughters. The god Enqi was well known for such activities, and could hardly turn against mankind for acting in ways that he himself did. Thus we have the opening of Gen Ch6:

> *"And it came to pass, when men began to multiply upon the face of the earth, and daughters were born unto them, that the sons of God saw the daughters of men that they were fair; and they took them wives of all which they chose."*
>
> Gen 6v1-2

Notice it uses the word *'took,'* implying sex by force, rape. And verse 4 takes it a step further by stating that another group of 'sons of God' married the daughters of man – by using the phrase, *'came in unto'* as opposed to *'took.'*

> *"There were giants in the earth in those days; and also after that, when the sons of God came in unto the daughters of men, and they bare children to them, the same became mighty men which were of old, men of renown."*
>
> Gen 6v4

The Sumerian tales, not only speak of poor sexual morals, but also tell of new guidelines for sexual intercourse amongst mankind. After setting a bad impression of sexual conduct, the gods, the Anunnaqi, established wedding ceremonies and taught mankind the meaning of compatibility, commitment and loyalty in marital relationships.[6] In particular, the gods taught their earth-descendants about genetic compatibility, as we shall explore shortly – albeit in accordance with our own times.

☒

Egiptian Viagra

So what about natural Aphrodisiacs? Well, the following may certainly explain a lot about rabbits: *'Lettuce is an ancient viagra, which can boost your sexual performance,'* scientists revealed recently. They say that it produces chemicals that were used by the *'Egyptians'* as an aphrodisiac.

Botanist Giorgio Samorini made the discovery when he solved a riddle that foiled experts for decades.

Min, the ancient Khemetian god of sexuality, is often depicted in bas-reliefs with a vegetable – and nobody knew what or why. But Samorini identified the plant as a bitter-leafed lettuce known as lactuca serriola. This initially confused him because, since Roman times, the sap produced by lettuce has been thought to dampen sexual desire. Emperor Nero is said to have eaten it to rid him of erotic dreams and Pliny the Elder wrote that lettuce can 'cool sexual appetite as well as a feverish body.' The Italian botanist carried out tests on the vegetable, which revealed that in small amounts the sap does, indeed, have a sedative effect. But in larger doses the substance – which includes a cocaine-like chemical – acts as a sexual stimulant. *'About 1g induces calming and pain killing effects,'* said Mr Samorini, editor of the botanical journal Eleusis. *'At the highest doses, 2g to 3g, the stimulating effects prevail.'* He added: *'This finally solves an ethno-botanical riddle and explains the association with Min and lettuce.'*

Many would agree that as informative as all this may appear, in today's societies, relationship compatibility has to be at the forefront of all discussions regarding marital relationships, let alone sexual relationships.

○

Ch.5

Compatibility and Relationships

Because the subject of compatibility is a very sensitive one, particular for those of the Hip-Hop community, it tends to confront us. Should we be asked, *"Are you truly compatible with and for your partner?"* It makes the hair on the back of our neck stand up, as we cringe due to a flash of reality that maybe we are not in a fully compatible relationship.

Most people fall into love relationships for the wrong reasons, though many of them may last many years. The same applies for people who choose to go into business with another; compatibility is very important, in so far as having common goals and agendas – not to mention trust. But first things first, that is, make sure you get into a relationship for the right reasons. I'm using the word 'right' loosely as a relative term. I mean 'right,' relative to the larger purpose you hold in your life. As stated, most people enter relationships for the wrong reasons – to fill gaps, end loneliness, and bring themselves love or to have someone to love – and these are some of the better reasons. Others do so to salve their ego, end their depressions, improve their sex life, recover from a previous relationship, or, believe it or not, to relieve boredom. None of these reasons will work in the long run, and unless something dramatic changes along the way, neither will the relationship.

We ought to take a journey back down memory lane into our past relationships, (as I have done,) and get *present* as to why we actually got involved with those people. Is it just because we fell in love? Most of us will find it difficult to remember the exact reason why we actually started a particular relationship. We tend to only remember what we decided about the relationship and not what actually happened. What we decided is based on an emotional interpretation of what actually happened.

For most people, love is a response to a need for fulfilment. So it is very easy to fall in love but extremely difficult to think in terms of the longevity of the prospective relationship. Too many warning flashes and signposts pop up and smack us in the face.

The first analysis ought to be one of compatibility, and, the second, one of relativity. This also depends on what our bigger goals in life are.

Now, let's take our esoteric understanding of 'relating' a notch higher.

¤

In creating that which is *"here"* and that which is *"there"*, God made it possible for God to know Itself. So God created *relativity* – the greatest gift that God could give Itself. Thus, *relationship* is the greatest gift God could ever give to us. From the No-*thing* sprang the Every-*thing*. First there was the first *thing*, then, there was the second. The period that is taken to travel from the *thing "here,"* to the *thing* over *"there"* became measurable, thus we have the creation of *time* and two *relative* points, therefore relationship. God knew that for love to exist – and to know itself as Pure Love – its exact opposite had to exist as well, and this we call fear. Everything that Love is not we experience through fear.

There is no "hate" in reality, only fear of not having Love, and the discomfort of this fear creates the illusion of hate. In the moment that fear existed, love could exist as a thing that could be experienced.

Just as humans have chosen to personify Pure Love as the character God, so have we chosen to objectively personify fear as the character called the devil. We therefore have many mythologies and folklore that teach of this creation of duality – with episodes of conflicts between good gods and bad gods, the forces of light and dark, etc.

In our relationships we have similar conflicts.

We all talk about how we feel love for, or, feel love from our partner. But is this a reality, or is it a misinterpretation of emotional responses to biological stimuli?

☿

The feeling of Love

So why exactly do we *fall* in love? The soul of our very be*ing* yearns for a feeling, one only attained through physical life and living. The soul does not seek knowledge of what Love is for it already has that knowledge, since the Universal Soul through Spirit, is indeed created out of Unconditional Love. So the soul in its earthly embodiment seeks to experience through feeling, sensation, and therefore e-motion, what Love is. Your soul's ultimate desire is to feel and experience the highest feeling of love ever possible. That is its purpose.

Knowledge of love is conceptual, but the feeling is experimental (or experiential) says Neale Donald Walsch, in his book *'Conversations with God.'* The highest feeling is attained when there is complete union with All that exists. It is the great return to Divine Truth and Divine Reality that the soul seeks. This beloved, is the Presence of Perfect Love.

Love is not emotional nor is it the absence of emotions. It is rather like the colour Black, which is the collective of all colours. Love is therefore the collective of all emotions – care, hatred, anger, lust, concern, covetousness etc. Thus for the soul to experience Perfect Love it must first experience <u>every</u> human feeling, sensation. Ask yourself these questions: "How can I have compassion for that which I don't understand?" "How can I forgive in another that which I have never experienced in myself?" "How can I be right if I don't know what wrong is?" However, and this is the key, out of every decision the soul makes, for example, to go left or right, up or down and so on, its task is to select the best of the two possibilities, and, never condemn that which is not grand. This is a big task, and can possibly take many lifetimes to master.

> *"Condemnation without investigation is the height of ignorance."*
> Albert Einstein

We are quick to judge our feelings about situations as "bad," "wrong" or "not enough," rather than to bless what we have as a Divine lesson. Sometimes we do worse than condemn our own feelings, and prefer to seek to do harm towards that which we do not choose. We seek to destroy it, or at least to prove it wrong. If there is a *person*, *place* or *thing* with which you do not agree or, does not agree with you, you deploy an attack. If there is a religion that doesn't believe in what you believe, you oppose it. If there is even a thought from another that contradicts or challenges yours, you ridicule it. This creates very serious errors within your soul, for it causes a bias toward only one side of the created universe. So how can we even begin to understand 'our own side' if we completely reject 'the other side'? These are the exact implications of sensed incompatibility in our love relationships. 'The Science of Love in the Making' has therefore gone completely out the window.

How can we have a truly loving relationship with another if we are not mentally strong enough to deal with opposition? To deal with opposition is simple, but definitely not easy. The first thing is to realise that there is no opposition in reality – situations just are. For every action, personal characteristic, place, event or thing, that occurs in the manifested world, there is an equally opposite one. Or, according to the Kaballah, for any *thing* (universes, gods, men and beasts) to be manifested in the lower realms of the Astral Light, there must be two possibilities for it to occur and exist. The extremeness of the two possibilities creates the illusion that they are in opposition. Lack of awareness of these basic spiritual principles can cause serious disturbances within our soul, which on the face of our daily behaviour creates enmity between our self and our loved ones.

We have forgotten what it is like to be loved without condition. We do not remember the experience of the Unconditional Love of God. So we try to imagine what the Love of God must be like, based on what we see of love in the world, to do this we mimic media informed love relationships. An associate of mine once said in jest, *"Love is a concept created by Walt Disney to give people hope."* Indeed, it is the human being that has created the concept of love which surrounds a fear-based reality, rooted in the idea of a fearful, vengeful God. We have projected the role of parenthood onto God. We remember how our own parents would scold us for being disobedient and so on and thus come up with a God who judges, rewards and punishes, based on how good He <u>feels</u> about what we have been up to.

Having thus created an entire belief-system about God based on human experience rather than spiritual realities, we have also created an entire new reality around love. Every action taken by human beings is based in love or fear, – not just those actions in our love relationships.

Decisions affecting business, industry, politics, religion, education, war, social structures and so forth are all rooted in love and fear. It seems that the fear-based decision wins more often than not, why is this? We have been taught to live in fear. The Western system does not propagate love in all aspects of its societies. We have been taught about the 'survival of the fittest, the victory of the strongest and, the success of the cleverest.' Precious little is said about the glory of the most loving.

Compatibility in relationships in ancient times was based on a more scientific approach, particularly in Royal and Monarchy systems. Priests used genetics to screened Royal couples to determine whether or not they would be compatible in terms of having children, since ultimately this is what marriage is all about. This was an actual science, known today as eugenics.

☒

<u>Choosing a mate or partner</u>
Eugenics by definition is, *'the study of methods to improve the mental and physical characteristics of the human family by choosing who may or may not be compatible to marry.'*

Today many couples do carry out blood tests before marrying, but only to screen for diseases or impurities, never solely for procreative compatibility.

I married Louise, my seventh significant relationship and the mother of my twin boys, Sahleem and Sahlee, when I was 25years old. The marriage lasted less than one year.

"What happened?" I hear you ask. Plainly and simply, and without going into why I chose to marry, other than the obvious reason, falling in love, we were not compatible. Nature also had something else in store I was unaware of. We both carried the sickle cell trait, a condition found amongst Caribbean and Afrokhan peoples. As carriers of the trait of the disease sickle cell anaemia we did not actually suffer the disease. However it meant that our children stood a very high chance of being born with the actual disease, and that is exactly what happened. In my wife's world at the time, the idea of having to deal with the potential suffering of two babies at once was a lot to bear and take on.

This put a huge strain on everything and thus our intentions of marriage and staying married faded drastically. There were also other incompatibilities present which I need not express here but, had I carried out a screening of my own blood and DNA, we probably would not have married, let alone had children. Marriage is indeed about children and the propagation of the human species, in the image and after the likeness of God.

The principle that we are working on here is Choice:

> *'Choice is the ability to recognise alternatives and possible consequences, thereby enabling the selection of*

that which is most desirable, admirable, and honourable – the ability to act in response to the recognised alternatives.[7]

Iyanla Vanzant

However, here is a fable about decision-making: There is a young boy who is having a dream about a motor accident takes place. The car is driven by his father, with his mother in the front passenger seat and himself in the back, and goes out of control and tumbles over a bridge and into a lake. Now here is the dilemma. The boy is able to save himself as he is a good swimmer, but can also only save one of his parents. What should he do?

He should wake up!!!

The lesson here is this: just because we are presented with a dilemma to make a choice between two things, doesn't mean that we actually have to opt for one or the other. Sometimes the best option is to not choose at all, and allow whatever is to be, to be. Decision-making in starting a relationship or, whilst already in a relationship, regardless of the nature of it, brings forth responsibility. The moment we decide to go 'east,' instead of 'west,' by spiritual law, the 'Law of Responsibility and Godliness' sets in.

> ## It is your God given right to take Responsibility for the events of your life

We have to take responsibility for our decisions and the outcomes of them. We have to accept that we automatically create the implications and the impacts of our actions through our choosing of what to do, and of what not to do.

The consequences of our decisions or our failure to choose, teaches us how to live in harmony with our Self and with others. God, the Higher Self, Conscience, the energy of the Divine Astral Light, always guides and protects us. It is, however, up to us to listen intimately to what the Higher Self is communicating. It speaks to us as feelings. It speaks to us as the need to understand and to grow, and to develop into a super conscious be*ing*. Sometimes the pace of life and nervous habits forces us to make quick decisions without listening to the suggestions of the Higher Self. However, awareness that we are in this situation helps. Just being aware of the Presence of the Divine Self and its guiding obligations strengthens us in our choosing.

When choosing a mate or partner, weigh all the possible alternatives, and evaluate all the possible consequences, then choose freely, for you will be responsible for the outcome – not your partner. Your partner will likewise be responsible for her or his decision-making on entering the relationship.

> **'Meantime relationships provided us with lessons that help us understand who we are, and prepares us for the ultimate experience.'**
>
> Iyanla Vanzant

Quick decision-making, which I have been well known for, without the intervention of inner thoughts, quickly teaches what works and what doesn't work in our lives. On the other hand, clearly focused choices grounded in self-awareness and trust in the Divine Astral Light, (God), reveals to you the Divine Truth and the Divine Reality of your inner knowing. All choices, whether forced or focused, resistant or courageous, will take you to a level of understanding that will ultimately affect the way you view life. This will influence the way you choose your mate or partner. Having the willingness to make choices promotes a willingness to grow and develop.

When we consciously choose growth over stagnation and fear, the Divine Astral Light of the universe supports us in the decision, by bringing us the lesson gently and lovingly. Stagnation and fear on the other hand goes against the most fundamental principle of the universe, and that is change, which is to grow. This way we miss the lessons that are presented by the Divine Astral Light, but rather we learn the ones presented by the gross astral light, the hard way!

Some say we live in a world dominated by *sin*, forces of evil that work against the betterment of humanity; forces that do not love nor understand love. But the word *sin* can also be seen as an acronym for, 'Self Inflicted Nonsense.' In reality no one individual can inflict sin upon you. Similarly, no one individual can do anything for you or against you; you create your reality as you progress through life, by the decisions you make. The matrix mentality is what we are dominated by; and it has created for us *'an 'Emotional Alcatraz,'* says David Icke. The matrix mentality is based around our not expressing our selves truthfully, as we are too worried and concerned about how others will feel. Just think of the amount of people around you, who you care about. Think of how you allow them to suppress what you want to do with your life because you are concerned by the way it will make them feel. So it is clear to see that the 'feeling of love,' 'choosing a mate or partner' and the fear of being brutally honest with everyone about your intentions, can create an emotional prison. Surely the Creator did not intend for us to create our own spiritual demise in this or any manner. No. It is us who, through so called free will, and through the desire to rule ourselves, have caused our own pain and suffering, just because what we call our feelings having 'love and fear' at its polar opposites.

Making the wrong decision in selecting a wife or husband can turn the marriage and the relationship into a prison sentence, and a family home into a prison cell, where no one, including the children, is able to express himself or herself freely. Please, don't get me wrong. I am not saying to mistreat people just because you feel like it, or to make peoples' lives miserable just for the sheer sake of it. I mean to express what you are, say what you think, live your uniqueness, without suppressing yourself because those around will not understand the real you. It means to stop living what *they* think you should be; and start being the way that you really *are*. If they can't handle that, that's their problem and they should find someone else who would suit them better. If they can't, and insist that you suppress the real you to suit them, then they are unaware unpaid gatekeepers of the emotional Alcatraz.

Usually we encounter these types of issues and problems where misinterpretations of conversation, poor communication occur.

Communicating with Love
The art of conversation; powerful communication; and charisma, create great interpersonal and relationship skills.

But how about approaching your loved ones, your friends, and even strangers for that matter, with Unconditional Love? Obviously not love, as in the desire to be with any and every body, but to approach with compassion, care and concern. It is to approach people as if you are God in the flesh. Yes, why not use God as your yardstick? Is this not what modern religion is all about? Aren't the Muslims using Muhammad and Allah as their yardstick? Aren't the Christians using Christ Jesus and God/Theos as their yardstick? Aren't the Jews using Abraham and Yahweh as their yardstick? In my understanding, that is exactly so. Whatever concept you choose to accept as the Creator of the universe, ought to be your mentor. This may take some practice if you are not already that way inclined.

You may choose to initiate yourself into higher levels of awareness, and indeed higher levels of communication with others. The Angelic Ones will congratulate and welcome you, but you still have to remember that ninety-five percent of the population within your environment are not on a spiritually aspiring path, let alone the same path as yourself. So you have to keenly develop, a way or ways, to have inspiring conversations with people who are on different levels of development; or are of different cultures and who have different past experiences, and different ideals.

To have the ability to communicate powerfully, in ways that they are "touched," and/or "moved," and/or "inspired" should be your intention.[A] As you can see, 'The Science of Love in the Making' is not just about sexual intercourse at all, that is only a very tiny part of the subject. Love as a subject is vast, in fact it is infinite inasmuch that everything *ad infinitum* is created out of Love. We therefore experience

---

[A] This principle I picked up from the Landmark Forum in Action seminar series.

Love in infinitude ways along the great magical and mystical paths.

> 'We are not humans on a spiritual journey. We are spiritual beings on a human journey.'
>
> Stephen R. Covey
>
> Author of, *'The 7 habits of highly effective people'*

Charles Swindoll said:

> *"We are all faced with a series of great opportunities brilliantly disguised as impossible situations."*

Relationships are everything; they are indeed disguised as opportunities for us to aspire spirit-ward. Relationships exist as communication between planets and stars, water and air, heat and cold, thought and energy, and constantly create and change the world around us. Relationships are literally what make creation possible and human relationships are an expression of this truth.

Through communicating and relating we learn and grow. But, if blueprint rules are laid down that dictate how a relationship should be, or the direction that it should go in, then, we are immediately building barriers to all other potential experiences and, therefore, greater understanding. The flow of life leads us into what we need to experience and with whom, in order to get to the next level, and this flow comes from within ourselves. Once we lay down the way it must be, *or else,* whether for ourselves or to impose upon others, we are challenging that flow, which may have other unforeseen plans for us. And, in situations like this, we may as well forget about sex magic and the unlimited possibilities therein.

○

Sex Magic
Many once thought that sex magic was an unsavoury and evil act. Modern thinking however concludes that this is not at all true. The idea that sex magic is evil came from the antiquated and malignant idea that women were, in and of themselves, somehow impure. Hence, any connection with women was sometimes considered to be 'taken with extreme caution.' Today we are capable of recognising that this is absurd.

Sex magic is a beautiful sacrament; a sacred ritual performed with a lover. Through this connection you and your partner can achieve communion with the Collective Unconscious, with the Divine Astral Light and the cosmic consciousness of the universe.

> 'When a man and a woman come together in the sacred ritual of sex, they are, at that time, the true image of the living God, male-female, mother-father, Pangenetor-Pangenetrix...'
>
> Jason Newcomb

Jason Newcomb teaches on the subject of sex magic. He says that sex magic can be performed by other combination of partners: male-female, male-male, female-female, or even by oneself – with varied results of course.

Sex magic is not complicated at all; it is relatively simple to understand. We must first recognise that within our genital fluids there is universal power to create life, and, with that understanding comes the knowing of the power to assist and make things happen in life. Whether it is to acquire wealth, peace with others, health improvement, or any other self-empowering experience, the required driving force is available through the power of orgasm. The moment of orgasm is one of pure cosmic power, which can either be directed to create life or directed to enhance life in whichever way we desire. Orgasm simply results in creation – but creation of what? You conscientiously choose.

In the coitus act, we are practically connecting the mental plane and the material plane as one single experience, with our emotional-body/soul acting as the path of communion. So through our emotions we can manifest that which we desire. There is unlimited possibilities and potential available through this sacred act. Yes really. Any purpose or objective can be adapted to a sex magic context.

However, this science should only be used if you have mastered the basics of mysticism. The Hermetic Order of the Golden Dawn and the Rosicrucian Order, as well as the New Hermetic systems bear witness to this science. Moreover, in volume 3 of *'The Mystical and Magical Paths of Self and not-self,'* you can explore the Spiritual Sciences of Nuwaubu as taught by the Ancient Egiptian Order.

In practice of sex magic, both participants must agree on a purpose or objective before the act commences. A talisman or amulet may also be useful in conjunction with the rite. All persons involved in the practice ought to share the same goal. This is very important. You and your partner should bathe consciously (together or separately), purifying the body with the element *water*, thus preparing the mind for the upcoming *fire*. Before beginning, some grounding or centering exercise should be carried out in preparation. I have included a very easy and simple grounding exercise below that can help to create an altered state[8] in preparation for the ritual. It is not intended for sex magic only; it can be used simply as a tool for preparing for the day ahead or for sheer relaxation.

However, after performing the exercise in the sexual context, sexual stimulation can now begin. Initially, the actual intention of the practice may be forgotten or ignored so as to focus on igniting the fires of passion. The stimulation procedure should be complete and passionate; once both are ready, intercourse can begin. At this stage, concentration must be turned back to the purpose of the rite, and remain focused throughout the entire operation. Direct your passion ecstatically toward the purpose of the operation, connect with your partner (unless you are alone) on all levels of passion, and direct your *will*. The passion must be extended for as long as possible, for no less than half an hour. Continue until it seems like orgasm is completely unavoidable. However, do not lose focus due to the actual orgasm. Instead, continue to focus on the purpose, and direct it through the ecstatic connection with your partner.

○̶

It may be useful to chant some sort of mantra to keep you directed and focussed. Orgasm will, in this case be simultaneous with your partner. It should be noted that the male can achieve a spiritual orgasm without actually ejaculating semen. Climaxing together indicates the intimate connection and the singularity of the act.

Grounding and Centering Exercise

1. Sit or lie down in a quiet place where you will not be disturbed for at least 20minutes.
2. Take a few deep breaths and allow yourself to get into a comfortable position.
3. Close your eyes and take a few-more long, slow deep breaths, totally settling into the position you have taken.
4. Notice the sensations in your body and readjust if necessary
5. Starting with your feet, progressively relax your entire body up to the crown of your head by feeling and visualizing a slow calming wave of energy moving soothingly up your body. You may mentally say, "My toes are relaxing, my feet are relaxing, my ankles are relaxing, etc."
6. When you have reached the crown of your head, you will be thoroughly relaxed. Feel the sensations of your body and relax any parts that have become tense again.
7. Mentally say to yourself that you are about to countdown from 20 to 1, and that, when you reach 1, you will be in a deep state of relaxation and focus.
8. Slowly begin counting backward from 20, mentally saying "20, and deeper, and deeper, I am relaxing deeper, 19, so much deeper, and 18, and deeper, and deeper, etc.," until you reach 1. When you reach 1 you will be in the altered state.
9. You may stay here for as long as you wish or go even deeper.
10. When you are ready to return to normal awareness, simply count upwards from 1 to 5, telling yourself mentally that you will awaken refreshed and relaxed.

At the very moment of orgasm the *will* must be entirely focused on the purpose of the operation, although consciousness may be temporarily lost in ecstasy.

As long as you and your mate are fully 'Present' to the science of the act, the sexual fluids can be gathered, for the final part of the ritual. This is according to Jason Newcomb. He says: *"A portion of the fluids must be placed on the talisman or amulet if there is one, and the rest must be consumed. This is absolutely important and must not be omitted from the ritual."*

The fluids, being the charged products of the operation, complete a true Eucharist. The combined fluids of the man and woman are a perfect substance, 'not living not dead, neither liquid nor solid, neither hot nor cold, neither male nor female.' It is one substance containing all possibilities. This is the Elixir of life.

It is said that, 'Once a person starts using sex magic, all sexual acts must be consecrated toward magic, or negative forces may be attracted due to the unbalanced forces of undirected sexual energy.' However, a true Kaballist will be intentionally balanced as a rule of thumb.

☒

Ch.6

Love and Relationship Archetypes

The contents of the Collective Unconscious are called archetypes. Carl Jung, the psychoanalyst, also called them dominants, the imagos[A] and the mythological or primordial images. But 'Archetypes,' seem to have won out over these. An archetype is an unlearned tendency to experience things in a certain way. The archetype has no form of its own, but it acts as the 'organising principle' of the things we see or do. It works the way that instincts work in Sigmund Freud's (another psychoanalyst) theory:

At first, the baby just wants something to eat, without knowing what it wants. It has a rather indefinite yearning, which, nevertheless, can be satisfied by some things and not by others. Later, with experience, the child begins to yearn for something more specific when it is hungry – a bottle, a cookie, a chicken leg, or a slice of pizza. The archetype is like a black hole in space: You only know it is there by how it draws matter and light to itself.

¤

[A] An imago is an optical representation of a *thing*.

Daddy's girl and Mummy's boy

There are clichés that say men usually try to find a girlfriend or wife modelled after their mother. And likewise, women try to seek out a boyfriend or husband modelled after their father. But then, when we study and analyse the theories of Freud and Jung, we discover that most of us seek out a partner based on our archetypical ideas of what our partners should be like. By this I mean: each and every one of us has an archetypical blueprint of motherhood, fatherhood, wifehood, husbandhood, childhood and so on. We carry around within us deep within our psyche, the qualities of each of these roles, with a misunderstanding that these should be the qualities that we should seek out. We say to our selves *"I would like to find someone who is like this... and like that..."* It very seldom occurs to us that these impressions are what we are to become and not necessarily what we ought to be looking for. Our inner being, our Conscience is telling us desperately, the way we ought to be in order to learn certain life lessons.

In volume 1 of MMSN, I wrote about the 'BE, DO, HAVE' philosophy, which I learnt from Robert T. Kiyosaki, author of the best selling *'Rich dad Poor dad'* series of books. We all want to *have* "this" and "that," and then "more." But, we miss the part that involves <u>*becoming,*</u> in order to <u>*do*</u> that which is necessary so that we may then <u>*have*</u> what we desire. It is a very simple mental-technology procedure.

Conscience speaks to us by way of the thoughts we have of the perfect lover. It speaks to us as thoughts of what a good parent entails, as thoughts of how our children should behave and indeed of how our friends are to treat us. But these thoughts are not to be taken as our expectations of others but rather as what are deepest potentials are, and therefore it is for us to manifest these archetypes as an example for others.

Instead, we pursue to effect change in others to suit our egos, thereby denying them the right to express themselves as how they really are and, on the contrary suppress our own potential in the process. This may sound monotonous to you as I rephrase this lesson in different ways. But I assure you that when these truths are put into practice, you will be exposed to unlimited power and self-expression.

You must understand that the archetypes are not biological things, like Freud's instincts. They are rather like spiritual demands. For instance, if you dreamt about long, conically shaped, solid objects things last night, Freud might suggest these things represent the phallus and ultimately sex. But Jung might have a very different interpretation. According to his way of thinking, even dreaming quite precisely about a penis might not have the slightest thing to do with some unfulfilled sexual desire. It is curious that in some ancient societies, phallic symbols do not usually refer to sex at all. They often symbolise spiritual power. These symbols would be displayed on occasions when the Ancestors are being called upon to increase the yield of corn or fish or to heal someone. The connection between the penis and strength, between semen and seed, between fertilisation and fertility are understood by some Afrokhan cultures.

☓

The Shadow and Persona
Jung, in his conceptual system also talks about sex and life instincts in general. He says that these are a part of an archetype called 'the shadow.' The shadow is derived from mankind's two-dimensional, animalistic past, when his concerns were limited to survival and reproduction, and were

not yet Self-conscious. It is the 'dark side' of the ego, and the evil that mankind is capable of is stored there. Actually, it is my belief that this aspect of mind that Jung speaks of is actually fundamentally inactive. That is, it is essentially neither good nor bad, just as we find within the animal kingdom. An animal is both capable of caring for and tending its young, as well as being vicious when hunting for food to feed its young. But, the animal does not actually choose to do either; it simply does what it does through instinct. It is therefore innocent and is not aware of it Self, or what we would call morality. From our human-world perspective, the animal world looks rather brutal, inhuman and cruel. We seek not to align with it and so these shadow aspects of ourselves, the survival tendencies, we tend to hide them away and pretend they do not exist. Symbols of this shadow include the serpent or the dragon, which quite interestingly guards the gates that lead us to our Collective Unconscious. So, next time you dream of wrestling with a demon, know that it may be yourself that you are wrestling with!

We cover up who we really are by what is called the **'Persona.'** The word is obviously associated with the words person and personality and comes from the Latin word *persona,* meaning a 'player's mask' – a player in the game of life in this case. So the *person* or *personality* is the mask we put on before we show ourselves to the outside world, and is definitely what we portray when we are seeking out a sexual partner, a business partner or a long-term relationship. At its best, on the face of it, it is just a good impression. It's the impression we all wish to fulfil that society dictates for us to become rather than express who we really are. It can also be the false impressions we use to manipulate peoples' opinions and behaviours. At worst, it can be mistaken by others and sometimes even by ourselves to be our true nature. Sometimes we really believe we are what we pretend to be.

A part of our persona is the role of male and female, or, of boyfriend and girlfriend we must play in our relationships. For most people that role is determined by their physical gender. But Jung, like Freud and others, felt that we are really bisexual in nature. Dr. Malachi has also taught this. He says (I paraphrase):

> 'When we begin our lives as foetuses, we have undifferentiated sex organs that only gradually, under the influence of hormones, become male or female. Likewise when we begin our social life as infants, we are neither male nor female in the social sense. Almost immediately – as soon as those pink or blue t-shirts go on – we become under the influence of society, which gradually shapes us as men and women.'
>
> Paraphrased from Dr. Malachi

Jung says that they are no known number of archetypes that one can remember and document. They overlap and easily melt into each other as and when needed. Other persona archetypes talk of the hermaphrodite, one that is both male and female in gender, and which represents the union of opposites, the merging of Yin and Yang. In some religious arts, Jesus for instance is portrayed as a rather feminine or as a *Yin* man. In China, *Kuan Yin* began as a male saint (the Budhisattva Avalokiteshwara), but was subsequently portrayed in a more feminine manner so that he is more often thought of as the female goddess of compassion. And again we have Akhenaton aka Amenhotep 1V, being portrayed as a tall man with breasts and wide hips.

Paul Simons

Ch.7

Love in Afrokhan Culture and religion

George James in the 1950s undoubtedly proved that Greek philosophy is stolen Egiptian or Khemetian philosophy. In fact, the very word philosophy is not even of Greek origin. It is Khemetian, from the words *Philo* meaning 'he who loves', and, *Sophon* meaning science, (also *Sophos* and *Sophia* meaning wisdom). Therefore the etymology of the word *philosopher* means 'he who loves science and wisdom.' History tells us that the ancient Neolithic Egiptians originated all the well-known sciences that are often attributed to the Greeks. This will be further elaborated upon in volume 3 of 'Urban Cries.' The term *philosopher* is also referring to a modern-day metaphysician – one who is calm, rational and temperate in her response to changes in nature and of life.

The Philosophy of Love
In Afrokhan and Asiatic cultures, the pursuit of love was based on the love to know the Self. The philosopher would strive with Unconditional Love, attention and devotion to understand and know her Self, as a microcosm of the macrocosm of the universe.

This, to the adept was what Unconditional Love was all about. The philosophy; the love of wisdom, impressed the importance, through application, that the return to the All, is to be in the exact same format in which we were originally differentiated as individual souls, as Unconditional Love. It was never about giving or receiving Unconditional Love from others. The doctrine determined that the only *thing* that is worthy of such Love is the Creator, NTR. Human love relationships only give us an idea of what the love of the Creator is like. The philosophy of love meant that the student would pursue Truth with love and commitment and, with the intention to study and internalise found truths into a functional mental tool for her Self-empowerment.

The seeking of love was a system of soul training says James in his book *'Stolen legacy.'* It is the path that raised the neophyte from human and mortal levels toward the level of virtue and God. James also described this system as the basis and purpose of the Egiptian Initiation System into the mystery schools, which was the first so-called salvation for man.

It ought to be noted here also that the famed Greek philosophers were only initiated into the lower of the lesser mystery schools. They were not mentally trained to deal with the fullness of even the lesser mysteries, let alone the greater mysteries. Therefore, we can see why today's society, apparently rooted in Greek philosophy and scholastic thought, is lacking love and care on a universal scale. If we are to re-establish care and love into the world, the powers that be, the preachers, rabbis and imams, the teachers and lectures, the scientists, physicians and parapsychologists, will all have to acknowledge the Afrokhan philosophy of Love, at the very least.

Throughout Afrokha and the Black cultures across the globe, we find these exact rites regarding Unconditional Love. It is at the foundation of every single Black culture for its people to exhibit love toward nature and to the universe as though their organs depended on it. This is not just a metaphor it is a reality. The practice of love in this manner is an Afrokhan sacred science, which includes sex magic as a vehicle to materialise certain desires, as well as, perhaps, to bring back a particular ancestor. Whatever one desires can be achieved through Love.

¤

A Blackman's Connection to God through the Blackwoman

Part_3

Paul Simons

144,000 Souls of Spiritual Nostalgia

Ch.8

In Conclusion

To wrap us this work, we will now essay into the metaphysical and neurological scientific principles of motion and e-motion, in an attempt to shift our understanding to a very powerful and fundamental paradigm – the world of Possibilities – freedom.

> **Emotion is created by Motion**
> Anthony Robbins

The Science of E-motion
It is now a scientific fact that emotion is created by motion. In other words, one can create desired emotions (sensations) by simply assuming specific physiological positions. This is only one method however. You can also create desirable sensations by way of mental stimulation. This might be through creative thought or through the memory of particular instances which conjure up the way you wish to feel now.

The spiritual philosophies of today (the last 50years) provide insight and understanding never before iterated to the general public. The meta-physical and the quantum-physical, and the new age esoteric principles, for instance, are profound in their abilities to explain the phenomena of human behaviour – in terms of love, and of how we relate to self and one-and-other. Science is therefore the means by which we can unravel the most mind-boggling metaphors and proverbs of many a scripture. For instance, Christ Jesus (Sananda) in his concept of the freedom, and of the infinite power and possibilities of a single grain of 'mustard seed' can only be quantified within the thesis and context of modern quantum science.

¤

The way in which one views the world is based upon what he or she believes to be real;[A] or, what is believed to be possible. Conventional science, for many decades taught us that the smallest indivisible unit of life is the hydrogen atom. Then we were told that that is not quite correct that the atom itself is made up of sub-units called hadrons and corpuscles. Hadrons are any combination of quarks such as protons and neutrons.[B] Corpuscles are classified as the sub-units of electrons and ions. Even this was also realised, also not to be entirely correct.

In fact, the smallest, the essential *stuff* of life and existence, is the substance of thought itself. The common esoterical term for this essential stuff is *ether*. So the *sub*-sub-unit of life and existence is nothing but a mist of randomly located etheric stuff, mentally arranged to suit a specific intent, that is, manifested objectively as the material world we view today.

¤

As above so below. As within so without…

[A] The Film: 'What the Bleep do we Know' makes this fact very clear
[B] See MMSN vol.1

The time is Now...

The sub-units of the brain work in exactly the same way as the sub-units of the Universe. Our neurons, the nerve cells that make up the brain and nervous system mimic how the Universe is created, manifested and thus perceived. Each neuron cell represents a bank of memory – like an envelope that holds the data of a specific experience. This experience doesn't have to be a physical one; it can be a mental one. In other words, the brain does not know the difference between what it holds as information, as something that originated from a thought (above-within), or if it originated as an actuality (below-without). The receptors of the neurons behave in exactly the same way in both cases when it receives information to be stored. So the brain, in what it perceives, does not understand the difference between what it is experiencing of the outside world and what it experiences from memory or creative thought – because the visual cortex processes information in exactly the same way in every case.[9] Similar to a television screen – it does not know the difference if the program is coming from a DVD player, a Video player, or from over the airwaves. The tube processes its received information in the same way, every time.

Any computer programmer or software writer will agree that a computer functions in a comparable way to the brain. A computer stores its information in RAM or ROM files called registers – akin to the storage cells of the brain called neurons. It makes no difference to the computer's registers whether the information comes from the outside world: a keyboard, or if it came from another register within the operating system. The read/write functions are exactly the same in both cases.

So here's the big question: what is more real, in terms of what we perceive? Is it the visions of the inner world or is it the visions of the outer? Interesting, isn't it?

And as said above – how we actually perceive the world is fundamentally based on what *we believe* to be possible.

Let us take a television camera for example. The camera (the observer) in a manner of speaking perceives the object (the observed) as exactly what it is without prejudice. It does this unconditionally, since it has no intents or purposes. It is free of objective observation; free of interpretation; and free of opinion. What you see is what you get.

But for all intents and purposes, the human perceives the object within a particular context. The context is created around the person's belief systems. These belief systems create neuron-nets within the brain to substantiate and to maintain the belief. The neuron-nets, when disturbed, when an activity of the outside world is experienced, sends signals to the limbic system of the brain, which then creates chemical reactions within the nervous system. This we experience as emotions, sensations.[10]

⌀

So then what are emotions?
"Energy in Motion…" (Dr Malachi)

> **An emotion is but a feeling that confirms what we believe to be the truth about some*thing*.**

Our thoughts create memory patterns within the brain. Each neuron cell has the potential to interconnect to every other neuron cell in specific patterns, like grooves on a music record. These possibilities are infinite. Our belief systems therefore create our ideals of what is right and wrong, good and bad, etc. Our nervous reactions to limbic stimuli create emotional responses that strengthen these beliefs.

What a palaver!

Let me try and practicalise some of this for you. Some time after the break-up of my marriage with Louise, I met Nadia. Guys, ever had a woman say to you, *'Slow down, you are going too fast!'* Well for me, it was the reverse. Nadia was determined that I was the man she was going to marry. Her confidence about this scared me to wits end. A ten-foot pole would not have been long enough to keep her away. It would seem, in retrospect, that the Angelic Ones were desperately trying to show me that love and marriage was still a possibility for me. But I wasn't paying attention, and, I had to ask her to slow down, she was going too fast for me.

Also, my neuron-net programming was hard-wired; no one could tell me anything. I had been devastated, embarrassed, and fool-felt about the sudden collapse of my marriage. I was in no position to even consider a proper girlfriend, let alone marriage, again.

The 'Law of Projection and Attraction' was in full effect once again. I was sending out so much love at the time, that the universe gave it back to me through Nadia.

But in my world, I had developed a belief system that had me imprisoned within my own space, within my own be*ing*. I was blinded. I remember Nadia trying to tell me that she was not Louise and that I should try and get to know her for who she really is. She wanted me to simply put the experience behind me and move forward with my life. But I couldn't do it – although deep down I knew she was right.

I always believed that the Angelic Ones guided her to me. I mean, I know we all are guided in some way or another to be of service to others, but this particular experience was a no-doubter. I had prayed and asked God to show me a sign that life can go on, and Nadia's spirit and loving energy was my answer: *"Yes it can."*

We lived together for two years before I finally left. I just wasn't ready for such a serious commitment, so soon. I tried. Again I prayed and asked God why I couldn't have met someone who wasn't so demanding (in my perception, of course). God responded by granting my wish, sooner than expected.

> **Pray with an open heart.**
> **God will respond powerfully if your quest serves the Greatest Good for all.**

By that time of my life I was becoming more and more aware of my spirituality, and was just about starting to put certain principles into practice. Later, I began to realise that all the people of my past that I had had issues with, and used to complain about, were actually manifestations of complaints about myself. I learnt, through retrospect, that life as I experience it is but a mirror, a reflection of my inner being.

I realised my prayers were never really meant for the Greatest Good for all. They were almost always self centred – all about me-me-me; all about me, myself and I. I did not know or understand that lessons are to be realised and learned about our shortfalls before we receive our blessings.

Two more significant relationships follow... so hold on.

I wanted Nadia to slow down to a level that she wouldn't seem so demanding. But the truth is she wasn't really that demanding. It was my own interpretation of the way she was being that made me believe she was going too fast. Perhaps I was looking at a reflection of myself, in that the generation of my relationship with Louise, up to the point of marriage was very fast indeed. It ended with a crash.

The Ultimate Observer

By spiritual law, the way we view the world around us is but a reflection of what's going on within. Nadia's behaviour became significant in my perception of women, because I had very strong issues about the speediness of my own marriage. This implication probably goes deeper into my past – perhaps even into my past lives.

The Angelic Ones were showing me a situation within myself that was to be confronted and dealt with. I needed healing, but I was too stubborn to turn my outer-visions into inner-visions. I was not observing my experiences and my environment as a reflection of my inner ramblings. It turned out that my subconscious way of solving these silent issues was to eventually meet someone who would not be too pushy, in terms of their expressing love towards me. It was as though this future girlfriend of mine had to be neutral – one who would only act in specific ways when, and only whenever it was necessary.

Thus, as soon as I had moved away from Nadia, the ideal woman who would fit my subconscious magnet, Desiree, arrived like a smack in the face.

The unforeseen aspect of meeting Desiree was that I would *fall* in love with her, practically immediately. This wasn't a part of the plan. Topsy-turvy is not a strong enough term to describe this scenario.

Desiree, though unbeknown to her at the time, turned out to be a living example of principles I would be teaching about in the five years or so after our meeting.

She had a very strange way of being, to me. She related to her environment, the world and her associates as though she was an observer. She was *'in the world, but not of it.'* Desiree had such a level of mastery over her emotions that sometimes I would think that maybe she didn't know how to love, which was absurd of me. Without any previous knowledge or doctrine of the esoteric to go on, she knew instinctively how to behave effectively as a human being – to operate from in the present, to be in the Now, as opposed to living life based upon past experiences or based upon emotions.

I certainly did not understand how a woman could behave like that. I was intensely disappointed and discouraged. I mean, I was more used to women having extramarital concerns about their partners. For some men, I suppose this attitude reassures them that their woman loves them, wanting the man for herself. Desiree, in contrast, did not have a problem with my having female friends – and of course she had a few platonic male friends of her own. I didn't even know how to handle that.

This was about taking trust to another level, for me. But in her world, she did not see what the fuss was all about, and did not understand why I was making such a big deal about her male friends. But the reality was this. I was really questioning my own levels of trust, not hers. The way she was, was just the way she was. For, if in my own ideal world, men and women could love and trust each other unconditionally, and that would include me, then I would not have had a problem with Desiree. I would have embraced her with open arms exactly as she was. Instead, I sabotaged what could have possibly been a long-lasting relationship, by constantly telling her that she didn't love me and that she couldn't be trusted.

Desiree was the complete opposite of the type of women I would normally get into a relationship with. She definitely was not into Hip-Hop and R&B to the degree that I was. Her genre of music was Reggae and Lovers Rock etc. Everything about her was different from me it seemed.

☿

Retrospection is very powerful. It enables us to understand Self from an observational point of view.

Try now, to put yourself into retrospective mode, and think of the many relationships you have sabotaged because of your own ignorance.

Ignorance is not bliss: it is soul torture. Ignorance leads to lack of awareness of Self. This in turn slows down the process in which the soul acquires the necessary lessons for its ascension. We receive these lessons when we learn to become Present, as an observer of our circumstances. Start to become Present to the more significant relationships of your past. Without judgement, simply review them to learn the lessons that you were being taught, especially if you were not aware of them at the time. Thank the Angelic Ones for the revelation. Then you can observe the least significant relationships and do the same.

If there are unresolved issues with past partners, you will have to confront them. This can be done by a simple telephone conversation. The objective is not to blame or make him or her wrong, but rather to speak of yourself only. Speak of the way you behaved, and of the impact it has had on your life ever since. You must also raise any positive aspects of the person or relationship you can remember. To close, you ought to talk about the possibility of being a transformed human being. By this I mean you can tell your ex about how you have recreated yourself based on what was learned from the relationship, and how it positively impacts upon your social environment. Thank them for the experience. Then thank the Angelic Ones/God for the opportunity of the conversation.

As stated before, sometimes you may have to speak to some people at a higher level, you may need to contact him or her in spirit, through prayer and meditation.

It is time for us to get in tune with the Ultimate Observer.

The time is Now

The ultimate observer is the ultimate observer. It is the faculty within us that looks out into the beyond. It is the aspect of the Self that perceives persons, places, things and circumstances exactly as they are without judgement. The ultimate observer is therefore God itself. God observes the world through the eyes of his creations. So ignorance and knowledge are two opposing polarities. The ultimate observer is that which is Present to All that Is/Isn't.

Final Acknowledgements

I realised through my life coach training process that I am the one that creates my life – no one is to be blamed or given credit. Every experience I have had is in direct proportion to what I believe and focus on at the subconscious level.

As a final acknowledgement of the women of my life, I shall present to you my most unusual experience ever. About six to seven months after my split with Desiree, I met Hidiatu. She is of Nigerian descent, but was born here in the UK. Following on from Desiree, whom I consider to be emotionally well balanced, Hidiatu also took me by surprise; she was a whole different kettle of fish, as far as my experience of love was concerned.

By this time of my life, I had already been through many degrees and levels of personal growth and development within myself. But, I had never really had the opportunity of being tested. There is an axiom that says; *'A man should practice what he preaches.'* Hidiatu was to be the vehicle in which the Angelic Ones would use to test my beliefs and faith within myself. I was well versed in metaphysical principles, and principles of human behavioural shaping.

I also knew that much of what I would speak about or teach on, in terms of personal development, I had fallen short of myself. I remembered Dr Malachi once saying, *"When a man teaches others, passionately, he is really teaching himself."* Hidiatu was not a particularly esoterically minded person and so I had taken on the task of being a teacher and inspiration for her. Her life-situation had been one of much pain and great disappointment regarding men. I immediately saw this as an opportunity to help someone realise that life is far simpler than we make it. I was quick to wear my 'Life Coaching' cap. I wanted to get her to realise her true potential as a human being, as a child of the Creator, and, as one who does not need a *partner* in life in order to feel alive. It turns out I was really talking to myself. I understood these principles technically, but it never really occurred to me how much healing I actually needed myself. My aim had always been to help others.

Therefore my commitment to Hidiatu had been to help her complete her past life-situation, more so than having a commitment to her as her partner.

Hidiatu was a direct reflection of me. Every single way in which I believed she needed to be developed was, in fact, a direct reflection of my self. The lessons I was giving were actually for the both of us. I became a channel through which the Angelic Ones were trying to help us both heal.

The significance of meeting Hidiatu was that through the experiences within our relationship, I became a hugely transformed human being, and, I am still growing and developing as you read this.

Hidiatu displayed such a level of integrity, commitment and endurance that an observer could only describe this as Unconditional Love. So I take this opportunity to acknowledge her for who she is as a person. She is a perfect example of one who displays Unconditional Love.

I was reluctant to open up to her in ways that I had done with previous women. This is because I had entered the Present-Now. I had learnt how to become an observer of my thoughts and emotions, without identifying with them, and without reacting to them. I became fourth dimensionally Present. As exciting as this may sound to you, for me, it was initially a very lonely place to be. I felt no one could relate to me anymore, and vice versa.

It was also a little frightening for me upon entering the Present-Now, since anything is possible within this state. I was frightened because indeed ANYTHING WAS POSSIBLE, and, particularly because Hidiatu was very receptive and cooperative with me regarding my intentions. So, I felt I ought to be very careful of what I declared in terms of the direction of the relationship. It wasn't just about the relationship. I was in a 'zone of void' for some time, concerned how to move forward with my life in general, and, with my pursuits for financial independence.

☿

I had been bombarded with countless business opportunities, and was present to the possibility of being successful in any of them. I was also very Present to the 'Law of Integrity and Manifestation.' These principles were important to me because the issue of money is, for me, a high priority, particularly considering the welfare of my children.

With regard to Angie, the mother of my first son, Levelle, I became her enemy, in a manner of speaking. She was deeply disappointed by the fact that I was not financially supportive regarding our then young child. I would often use my not having much money as an excuse, to be not around much. The truth is, I wanted to be supportive but lacked the know-how, or the drive, to be consistent. I later learned that it was not the lack of money that was the problem, but rather my attitude toward money in general. Of course, the level of belief within myself, and my being able to manifest whatever I wanted out of life, in terms of financial gains, was not sufficiently developed.

I was lacking integrity big time.

However, I acknowledge her for taking on our son as mother and father. She had done a fantastic job, practically on her own. Many single mothers can relate to this no doubt. I also acknowledge my ex wife Louise in the same regards. She has taken on the twins, Sahleem and Sahlee, with their sickle cell anaemia disease, as well as her three girls. I give my sincere apology to both women for my not being a consistent father in the beginning.

I would also like to acknowledge all the less significant relationships in my past – and those names unmentioned. For any injustice I had caused/created, I am truly sorry. I am also thankful to the Source for allowing me the opportunity to meet all the wonderful people I have had the priviledge of meeting, throughout my life. All of you are indeed a projection and a reflection of my self and ultimately the source.

¤

A New Beginning
My life-situation up until when I started to write this book was very uncertain and at times somewhat shadowed. Like most people, I spent many years believing that my life situation with regard to love and relationships was actually my true life, and in some relationships I believed I was really experiencing true Love, but then, eventually, the passion died. True Love has a way of showing it self to us; it turns up at the most unexpected of times and it brings the means for change and transformation along with it. These means are available to all of us, if we are open hearted enough to let Love step in and start the healing process. This is absolutely

necessary if we want to restart our lives, if we desire a chance to get a clear, unveiled view of exactly where we want to go.

Many people are brought up to believe that true Love is about giving *all* our energy over to someone else and being completely devoted and trusting. This is not, however, what my life experiences have taught me. I have learned through my experience of life that true Love is about allowance. Allowance is a very high spiritual faculty. If you can just *be* and allow people to *be* exactly the way they are without prejudgement or blame, then you are on your way toward Self-realisation and Ascension. By allowing a situation to *be* exactly the way it presents itself, whether or not you are justified to blame or credit someone else, the Universe empowers you to see a much bigger and clearer picture of which the situation you face is but a tiny attribute. These are very powerful concepts.

With regard to music, it has been, and still is, today, a fundamental medium that somehow helps people to "allow", at least for a while. How may times have you ended up in a predicament that was just too much to handle, but, by taking time out and immersing yourself in the mood and vibrations of a song you love, you then find yourself to be forgiving and allowing. Many of us experience this with music.

What about keeping the passion alive? Monotonous routines in a relationship can eventually kill the passion, so this calls for very wise and skilful manoeuvres on a periodic basis.

The following chapter presents ten pages of very simple but effective principles that can assist us to keep the passion alive in our relationships. Be courageous and make use of them. Some of them may be new ideas to you while others can be seen as just plain common sense.

Life is about always starting afresh, beloved. If we are not changing and transforming toward the new then we are, according to natural law, going in the other direction. Change is a prerequisite for growth. This is the law.

Marriage for me when I was growing up has been, and still is, the ultimate experience of Unity, Integrity and Commitment whilst living on earth. The Universe has taught me some very valuable lessons, including that marriage helps people to begin to realise who they are and what is expected of them.

So I end this by saying: may you grow in love and passion and enjoy God's special gifts. You deserve it.

¤

Ch.9

Keeping the Passion Alive

Generally speaking, when a man's emotional and passionate needs for love are not satisfied, he becomes entranced with sex, while a woman tends to become captivated with romance.

※

Since contemporary women increasingly can provide for themselves, they want more from a partner than helping to take care of the family.

※

For men or women, having an affair is ultimately an attempt to fulfil our need for love.

※

Forgiveness is very powerful and can solidify a loving bond for ever.

Paul Simons

The most important aspect about attraction is that we are different. By taking the time to make sure that we avoid emotional role reversal, we can maintain the attraction we feel to each other.

※

Having to give up who we are to please our partners ultimately kills the passion. By seeking to resolve our differences without having to deny our true selves, we ensure lasting attraction.

※

When passion is sustained, our curiosity and interest in our partners also grow over time.

※

Working with our differences is a requirement for keeping the passion alive.

※

For a woman to remain attracted to a man, he must be in touch with and express his male side. But if he suppresses his male side to be in a relationship with her, he will eventually lose her attraction to him.

*

Without taking deliberate steps to nurture her female side, a woman today will tend to automatically stay in her masculine side and unknowingly sabotage not only her relationships but her relationship with herself as well.

*

Loving your partner does not mean spending all of your time together.

*

Living with the same person can, over time, eventually become very boring if they are not regularly changing. Staying fresh is crucial for both partners in a marriage.

Paul Simons

※

Just as listening to a favourite song a hundred times in a row makes it grow stale, so also may our partners become boring if they do not grow and change.

※

Just as physical growth is so obvious in our children; we must always continue to grow emotionally, mentally and spiritually.

※

When a relationship does not allow us to grow, the passion between the two people begins to fade.

※

Too much time together can also make a relationship commonplace and devoid of mystery. Enjoying other friends and activities means that you can always bring back something new to the relationship.

*

If a woman does not feel safe in talking about her feelings, she will eventually have nothing to say. Creating the safety for her to talk freely without her having to fear rejection, interruption, or ridicule allows a woman to thrive in a relationship.

*

It is crucial that a man experience repeatedly that he can make and is making a difference in a woman's life.

*

A woman feels loved when she feels that a man's love is consistent.

*

Over time, a woman can continue to trust and love her partner more if he is a good listener.

As a man begins to understand how to listen in an attractive way that his mate can appreciate, listening and sharing stops being a chore and becomes an important ritual.

With open lines of communication, a woman will continue to grow.

When a man does not feel appreciated he also stops growing.

It is important to schedule special occasions. If a man creates special times when a woman can get out of the routine, she is free to feel nurtured.

Doing something special on those days for her frees her from feeling overwhelmed by life's repetitive responsibilities and assures her that she is loved.

※

One of the chief killers of passion is routine. Even if you are comfortable in your rut, it is helpful to break out of it from time to time.

※

Ultimately, what keeps passion alive in a relationship is growing in love.

※

When, as a result of living, laughing, crying, and learning together, two people are able love and trust each other more, the passion will continue.

*

When a man stops feeling a tender desire to please his partner, his tender feelings are automatically suppressed.

*

Slowly but surely, by continuing to successfully communicate and appreciate each other, that wall of suppressed feelings can come down and feelings can be fully experienced again.

*

To continue feeling our love, we need to feel; when we are not getting the love we need, but remain vulnerable to our partners, we feel pain.

*

Only in learning to reach out for love and ask for what we want in skilful ways can we really heal the pain.

When a man does things without a woman having to ask, she feels deeply loved. If he forgets to do them, though, a wise woman graciously persists in reminding him by asking in a non-demanding manner.

※

To be really good friends in a relationship requires a balance of autonomy and independence.

※

Just as communication and romance are the primary means for a woman to experience love, sex is the primary way for a man to connect with love and passion on an ongoing basis.

※

The real test of love is when we can be our partner's friend, and give without any expectation of return.

Paul Simons

*

For a woman to feel friendship for a man it means that he can be relaxed about her getting upset.

*

Being our partner's friend means never trying to change their mood or taking personally when they are not feeling the way we want them to.

Appendix

This section is presented to give a little more light on some on the terminologies and phrases used within this book:

Appendix A

The Law of One and Interconnectedness

This affirms that there can be no separation from the Creator; therefore, there is no separation between man and the *persons*, *places* and *things* of his life.

[Adapted from 'The Distinctions of Nuwaubu'; Nebu Ka Ma'at][11]

The Principle of Oneness affirms our connection to every manifested part of the universe. It affirms our interconnectedness with 'All that Is.' In the ancient Lemurian and Atlantean civilisations, this is known as 'The Law of One.' With regard to this, in the fifth dimension and above there is only one spiritual law. We are all one. We are all part of God. The Distinction of Oneness is about accepting everyone and everything as they are, without judgement. This includes your self!

Whenever you set out to do a task, stop for a few seconds and just get Present to the reality that your forthcoming actions will affect everyone else, at least those in your immediate environment.

Be mindful of the protective barriers you put up to defend your self; they prevent you from being one with others. Think of the positive and negative implications of your intentions. Then ask yourself the question: "Will the outcome of my act serve the greatest good for all?" Your highest intuition will respond with the correct answer, so listen keenly without judgement.

Appendix B

The Law of Intention and Karma

This affirms that, as a man thinks, intends and does, so he is. His deeds will eventually come right back to him in exactly the same proportion as he gave them out.

[Adapted from 'The Distinctions of Nuwaubu'; Nebu Ka Ma'at][12]

Intention is the number-one driving force for all our heart's desires.

As above so below. The mind of The All – the Universal Mind, shares its Power with each and every one of us. Whatever the Universal Mind intends manifests. We individually have that same potential. Whatever we clearly intend, also manifests. There can be no doubt in our intentions; we will sabotage the intended outcome. So our affirmations must be one hundred percent doubt-less.

If you *want* to go swimming, you can be deterred. If you *intend* to go swimming you will overcome all obstacles in order to fulfil your intention. Similarly, the person who intends to get married is more likely to do so than the person who just hopes to get married one day. Intention creates tension – like an archer who pulls his bow back and holds it 'in-tension.' He then releases the arrow, aimed at his target with great force.

Whatever your aims are in life, the Universe will back your Intention with great force. This is regardless of the intended Polarity of your outcome (positive or negative).

Appendix C
The Law of Projection and Attraction

This affirms that what we project out in energy comes right back to us in the form of *persons*, *places* or *things*. For instance, one may attract the conditions of poverty because he sends out that kind of energy in terms of negative thoughts of being poor. He therefore finds himself constantly surrounded with undesirable mediocre circumstances.

[Adapted from 'The Distinctions of Nuwaubu'; Nebu Ka Ma'at][13]

A Projection is a presentation of images. The eyes do not actually see images, the visual cortex within brain does. But, what we perceive through the lens of the eyes is but a reflection of light waves we send out, or *project*. The way we experience the world is also based on the fundamental energies we subconsciously emit or transmit.

Your exercise is to practice the Principle of Projection. By way of conscious observation of your thoughts and emotions, you become Present to a higher awareness.

From this space, you can consciously project Love, Affinity, Appreciation, Gratitude, or Grace and so on. You can do this with any given circumstance. By design you can create any desired type of magnetic Attraction, simply by way of what you project.

The Principle of Attraction works hand in hand with Projection. Simply put, we attract whatever we project. Many people speak of finding the perfect partner, but fail to see the benefits of becoming the perfect partner themselves.

Therefore, if we focus on the type of partners we do not want, this is exactly what we will get. This is because the subconscious mind is not receptive to positive or negative desires. It simply proceeds to manifest whatever we focus on. Unlike the conventional 'N' or 'S' poles of magnetic attraction, like minds attract!

Whatever you choose to manifest in your life, whether it is a type of person, a type of *place* or *thing*, you must, in the Present-Now, mentally create the desired outcome of how things would be for you. This sets up a chemical reaction between the limbic and the hypothalamus regions of the brain, therefore producing specific neuro-hormones. This, in turn, correspondingly, sets up your be*ing* in a synergistic-magnetic manner to actually attract your desire to you.

However, the way you feel about your circumstances, whether it is desirable or undesirable, is actually a Reflection of your inner be*ing*.

Appendix D

The Law of Grace and Mercy

This affirms that unconditional forgiveness and compassion dissolves karma and reaps blessings.

[Adapted from 'The Distinctions of Nuwaubu'; Nebu Ka Ma'at][14]

Grace is an energy band available for us to tap into. Its frequency is very close to that of Blessings. We can give and receive Grace, just as we give and receive Blessings, at our own will.

When we align with these energy bands, we can end pain, illness, misery, famine and wars. Our soul has accepted the challenge of incarnating on planet earth at this time to either give or receive Grace and indeed Blessings. It is up to you then to choose your position, or at least align with your Higher Self to recall your mandate to memory. Negative karma does not have to be endured; you can dissolve it through the Grace of God.

Every time you open you heart with Compassion, Empathy and Love, unconditionally, you emanate an energy that grants someone else Grace. The Universe also grants you an inflow of Divine Love in the process. Why not take this way as your way of be*ing*?

By invoking and conferring Grace you can transmute negative emotions, heal relationships and the physical body. Through the power of Grace you defy karma.

Mercy is another Divine energy that also dissolves karma.

Appendix E

The Law of Responsibility and Godliness

This affirms that by man taking responsibility for his thoughts, intentions and actions, he can master the affairs of his life. He is therefore able to respond to the experiences of his life appropriately and so we have 'response-ability'.

[Adapted from 'The Distinctions of Nuwaubu'; Nebu Ka Ma'at][15]

Responsibility begins with the willingness to be the cause in all the matters of our life. Our livs must be founded with integrity. Responsibility is not burden, fault, praise, blame, credit, shame or guilt. With Responsibility, there is no good or bad, right or wrong etc. There is only what *Is,* and our stand for what *Is*.

Being responsible starts with the willingness to deal with a situation from the position which suggests that you are the generator of what you choose to do; what you have and who you are. Responsibility is therefore a Grace you give your self.

Responsibility is: Response-ability; having the ability to respond appropriately to your life-situation.

The Affirmation is to differentiate between our life-situation, and our True Life. Many of you confuse your life-situation to be your actual life.

Your ongoing task is to take full Responsibility for your life-situation, in the world of time and circumstance, and, at the same time become Present to your True Life, which is in the Present-Now.

Responsibility is Godly. You connect to God when you take full Responsibility. You therefore live in constant Prayer.

Appendix F

The Law of Integrity and Manifestation

This affirms that *'As a man thinketh in his heart, so is he.'* Integrity is the key to manifestation. Manifestation is confirmation of Integrity. Whatever we believe to be a possibility we can manifest. The intensity of how we visualise that possibility strengthens the integrity of the intention for manifestation. Integrity and Manifestation are therefore to bring into reality a preconceived idea, regardless of circumstances.

[Adapted from 'The Distinctions of Nuwaubu'; Nebu Ka Ma'at][16]

The Principle of Integrity affirms that whatever we say we are going to do is as good as done. Integrity and commitment go hand in hand. One hand washes the other.

Commitment is: *'Doing the things you said you would, even long after the mood in which you said it has gone.'*

Without commitment there is no integrity.

The fact that you said: *"I will see you at 5pm sharp,"* when setting an appointment, you set up a challenge for your integrity. You have told your subconscious mind its mandate, which is to get you *there* on time. Now, if there is a problem, traffic for instance, you ought to get word to your friend/client as soon as you realise you are running late. This reaffirms your integrity.

If you fail to acknowledge your friend/client, then your integrity is out. When this failure is repeated it programs the subconscious mind to sabotage any forthcoming agendas. You therefore lack integrity, which becomes a lack of Unconditional Love.

Appendix G

The Law of Unconditional Love

This affirms that True Love is to love unconditionally – without any objective, reason or intention. Unconditional love for 'All that Is,' raises awareness of Self onto higher realms of be*ing* which aligns one with the Angelic Ones; those who help the Creator.

[Adapted from 'The Distinctions of Nuwaubu'; Nebu Ka Ma'at][17]

This is the Principle of loving without purpose, intention or reason. Unconditional Love is Pure Love – it is to love for the sake of Love itself.

When we are in Love, heaven rejoices. God's will is thus for us to take a stand for Love, which brings us joy, fulfilment and a sense of worth. God's host (the Angelic Ones) finds it difficult to access us through negative energy, which is lack of Love; they can only access us completely when we have taken a stand for the Love of God.

The ability to give without the tendency of wanting to receive something in return is almost inescapable for the majority of us. So the task then is to practice unconditional giving, – to present your self in service to others, fully, and for no reason whatsoever. The Universe will reward you with unlimited Love, Peace and Joy, which bestows Blessings upon you.

Inside the bosom of Unconditional Love anything becomes possible.

Appendix H

Afrokhan

[Adapted from 'Urban Cries Vol.1'; Paul Simons][18]

I chose to redefine the word *Africa* as Afrokha, simply to make a distinction between what Europeans are referring to, – and, the true essence of the peoples of the said continent. Afro, is referring to the woolly hair of our crown; it represents our Kingly-ness as opposed to kinky-ness. And the word Kha is the Afro-Egiptian term for the animating Spirit. We also have the definition of Afrokhan, where Khan means to rule; to be morally upright, it also represents the civilisers of the world.

In the European worldview, *Africa* is a term that describes a conquered and therefore divided and destroyed people. I have therefore denounced that title and redefined my own, which works well within my own view of Reality.

Appendix I
AfroCentricity

[Adapted from 'Legacy of the Black Gods'; Paul Simons][19]

AfroCentricity and AfroCentrism, (which I might add are coined European terms,) supposedly, terminologically speaking, the equivalent of Eurocentricity and Eurocentrism.

Many of us tend to get sidetracked using terms like African-American or African-Caribbean, not realising that these terms actually continue to divide us by what is called Geopolitics. We are politicised according to our locations as opposed to the heritage and legacy of our collective experience on Earth.

AfroCentricity on the other hand attempts to unite the many races of the world, (all people of colour so to speak,) into one centralised system of life and living, and in accordance with the Afrokhan worldview and the Divine order, Ma'at. In light of this, we must, therefore, continue to acknowledge the forerunners of this journey – those who have laid the foundation for writers like me and students like you and I to take this journey to the next level. So throughout my work I call on the lessons of Dr Malachi Z. York, Gerald Massey, Cheikh Anta Diop, Dr Yoseph Ben Yochanaan, Anthony T. Browder, Dr Henrick Clarke, Sista Dr Marimba Ani, Dr Richard King, Molefi Kete Asante, Elijah Muhammad, Malcolm X, Ra Un Nefer Amen, Louis Farrakhan, Wayne B. Chandler, Phil Valentine, Aris La Tham, Caroline Shola Arewa, Delbert Blair, Marcus Garvey, Richard King, George G.M. James, Bobby Hemmitt, Dr Frances Cress Welsing, Booker T. Coleman, Malidoma Patrice Somé, Dr Jan Knappert, Kwame Nantambu, Carlyle

Fielding Stewart III, Anthony Ephirim-Donkor, Queen Afua, Emefie Ikenga Metuh and so many others.

So why is AfroCentricity an important part of our journey today? When I say 'our,' I'm talking about the human family. It is so vital and important because our strength as a collective people lies within our unity. If we are to adopt a universal system of education leading toward the transmigration of the Afrokhan Soul, we, as the collective human family, will inevitably transcend all that inhibits humanity in the world of Eurocentricity.

AfroCentrism, therefore, is not a system that is intended to badmouth any other ism, but rather one that celebrates all that leads humanity toward a consciousness of unity. To this end, we must, at least, call on both the doctrines of the past and present in order for us to understand, universally speaking, where we are to go next.

Appendix J

The Chakras
[Adapted from 'MMSN Vol.1, Ch16'; Paul Simons][20]

The force centres of the physical body lie within the spiritual body and are also referred to as our core energy. These force centres penetrate the endocrine glands of the physical form and draw the solar and life force energies from the atmosphere and transduces/interpenetrates them through their counterpart glands. They are the seats of light and intellect, and are the etheric sockets in which the glands are plugged.[21]

"Core energy is the still point of our very existence, the hub around which the wheels of light known as chakras revolve. This central core links us to every living entity and connects us to our creator. The chakras unite us to our Ancestors, who

bestow blessings upon us. The wisdom of the past, present and future is revealed to us via the chakras. Through the chakras we find God – the 'gift of divinity' which lies at the very core of each human being" [Caroline Arewa].[22] The word Chakra is in fact a Hindu Sanskrit word meaning 'wheels.' From a scientific perspective the Chakras are significant vortexes of energy that superimpose each of the major endocrine glands. The endocrine system within the physical form is a system of glands that secrete their hormones directly into the bloodstream as opposed to via ducts. Hormones are chemical messengers that instruct the various organs and glands of the body to perform particular tasks. Each Chakra is represented by a colour based on the rainbow colours, starting from the Base/Root chakra going up to the Crown/Cranial chakra:

RED: Base: Khundalini: Root Chakra: Located at the base of the spine; contains the 8 primary cells that have all of the knowledge of creation and remain the only cells in your body that do not change in your lifetime. It grounds us in the physical world.

ORANGE: Spleen: Splenic: Located just beneath the navel, and is related to our sexual and reproductive capacity. Blockage manifests as emotional problems or sexual guilt.

YELLOW: Solar Plexus: Seat of Emotions; gives us a sense of personal power in the world. Blockage manifests as anger or a sense of victimisation.

GREEN: Heart Chakra: Blockage can manifest as immune system or heart problems, or a lack of compassion.

BLUE: Throat: Tied to creativity and communication; emits feelings of pressure when you are not communicating your emotions properly.

INDIGO: Third Eye: Pituitary Gland: Is the spiritual eye with the capabilities of looking Spirit ward.

PURPLE: Pineal Gland: Crown: Connects you with messages from higher realms; can be experienced as a pressure on the top of the head.

References of Notes:

[1] Dr Pamela Connolly, *Psychologies Magazine*, p39 (April 2006)
[2] Dr Malachi, (a) *The True Story of the Beginning*, p8-10 (b) *The Holy Tablets*, p717
[3] Wayne B. Chandler, *Sexual Energy* (Audio Cassette)
[4] Dr Malachi, *The Fallacy of Easter, (Scroll #105)*, p14-15
[5] Zecharia Sitchin, *The Twelfth Planet*, p364
[6] Dr Malachi, *The Marriage Ceremony, (Scroll #53)*, p39
[7] Iyanla Vanzant, *One Day My Soul Just Opened Up*, p101
[8] Jason Augustus Newcomb, *the new hermetics*, p73
[9] What The Bleep do we Know, *Documentary Film*
[10] Ibid
[11] Nebu Ka Ma'at, *Distinctions of Nuwaubu*, p18-19
[12] Ibid, p56-57
[13] Ibid, p40-43
[14] Ibid, p84-85
[15] Ibid, p62-63
[16] Ibid, p20-21
[17] Ibid, p22-23
[18] Paul Simons, *Urban Cries Vol.1*, p91
[19] Paul Simons, *Legacy of the Black Gods*, p5-6
[20] Paul Simons, *MMSN Vol.1*, p208
[21] Dr Malachi, *The Holy Tablets*, Ch7
[22] Caroline Arewa, *Opening to Spirit*, p3

Index

A
Aesthetics
   Of Hip-Hop, 33, 37-38
Afrokhan, 33, 44, 67, 85-86, 121
   Cosmologies, 56
   Culture, 23, 47, 81, 84
Afrocectricity, 32, 122-123
Aphrodite, 55-56
Archetype(s), 79-81, 83
Atlantis,
   Atlantean, 114
Attraction, 8, 11, 33-36, 93, 106-107, 116-117
Awareness, 24, 36-37, 46, 51, 65, 69-70, 72, 77
   Of self, 97, 120
   Higher states of, 25, 36, 116

B
Black
   Blackman, 20
   Blackwoman, 20
   Community, 24
   Music, 9

C
Chakras, 49-51, 123-124
Compatibility, 59-62, 65-67
Conscience, 46, 52, 69, 80
Consciousness, 38, 50, 74, 78
   Duality, 54
   Higher states of, 47
   Polarity, 52
   Unity, 123
Creation, 48, 52-53, 56, 62-63, 73, 75, 98, 124

D
Divine, 39-40, 44, 46, 49, 69-70, 74
   Blessings, 22
   Lesson(s), 21, 25, 64
   Love, 52, 118
   Mercy, 21, 30
   Order, 48, 122
   Reality, 51, 63-64, 70
   Truth, 51, 63-64, 70
Doctrine(s), 20, 24, 34, 85, 96, 123
Dr Malachi Z. York, 48, 83, 92, 99, 122

E
Egiptian(s), 59, 75, 84-85, 121
Egyptian(s), 59
Elijah Muhammad, 122
Embodiment, 63

F
Farrakhan, 27-28, 33, 122

G
God(s), 22, 25-27, 39-41, 44, 51-52, 54, 56, 58-59, 62-63, 65-66, 68-70, 72, 74, 85, 94, 98, 104, 114, 118-121, 124
   Communicating with, 38
   Connection to, 10, 25, 27
   Image of, 26, 67
   Sons of, 59
Goddess(es), 55-56, 83
Godliness, 11, 35, 68, 118

H
Hip-Hop, 15, 18, 22, 34, 97
   Community, 11, 61
   Culture, 11, 19, 24, 28-29, 33, 37-39

Index

I
Integrity, 11, 35, 37, 52, 100-101, 104, 118-120

J
Jesus, 32, 72, 83, 90

K
Karma, 11, 20, 35, 115, 117-118
Khemet, 46
   Khemetian(s), 59, 84
   Khemetic, 54
KRS One, 22, 39

L
Lemuria
   Lemurian, 114
Love, 6-11, 18, 25-26, 36, 44-45 52-57, 63-66, 70, 72-73, 84-86, 89, 93, 95-97, 99, 102-105, 109, 111-113, 116, 121
   Divine, 52, 118
   Falling in, 10, 30, 62-63, 67
   Feeling of, 63, 71
   Relationships, 22, 54, 61, 65-66, 85
   Unconditional, 7, 11, 36, 63, 65, 72, 84-85, 100 118, 120-121

M
Malcolm X, 33, 122
Mercy, 11, 21, 30, 35, 117-118
Mental, 10, 19-20, 23-24, 46, 52 66, 75, 80, 85, 89, 91
   Mentality, 15, 28, 70
Mind, 7, 31, 46, 51, 53, 76, 82, 89 116, 120
   Of the All, 115

   Universal, 46, 115
Music, 9, 15, 34, 36-39, 93, 97, 103
   Culture, 10, 19-20
   Musical Influence(s), 9, 18

N
Nuwaubu, 75, 114-120
   Nuwaubian Nation, 20, 24

O
Oxytosin, 6

P
Persona, 81-83
Personal Development, 15, 19, 23, 99
Personality, 82
Projection, 8, 11, 34-36, 93, 102, 116

R
Rap, 34
   Rapper(s), 22, 33
RnB, 15
   Culture, 10, 28-29
   Community, 11
Responsibility, 11, 21, 29-30, 32 35, 37, 68, 118-119

S
Self, 46, 65, 69-70, 81-82, 94, 97-98, 100, 114, 119
   Awareness of, 36, 69-70, 97, 120
   Expression, 22-23, 81
   Higher, 21, 36, 54, 69, 117
   Knowledge of, 84
   Realisation, 36, 103

Index

Sex Magic, 74-76, 78, 86
Sexual
    Energy, 46-47, 78
    Intercourse, 45, 49, 58-59
    72
    Mantras, 48
Soul(s), 36-37, 63-65, 84-85, 97,
    117, 123
    Mate(s), 53
    Music, 15, 18, 22
    Twin, 53-54
Spirit, 22, 26-27, 39, 46, 49, 63,
    73, 94, 98, 121, 125
Spiritual, 37, 47, 49-51, 53, 66,
    71-73, 76, 81, 89, 94, 103,
    125
    Body, 123
    Guides, 37
    Law(s), 7, 41, 68, 95
    Principles, 30, 38, 65
    Plane, 26
    Science, 75
    Spirituality, 23

T
Transformation, 23, 49, 102

U
Unconditional Love
    See Love
Universe, 16, 29, 39, 46, 52, 65,
    70, 72, 74, 84, 85, 91, 93,
    103-104, 114-115, 118, 121,

V
Venus, 55-56
Volition, 19

Y
Yin and Yang, 53, 56, 83

Lightning Source UK Ltd.
Milton Keynes UK
UKOW051145300112

186304UK00003B/280/P